THE
NEW
QUANTUM
MECHANICS

www.royalcollins.com

THE
NEW
QUANTUM
MECHANICS

Kevin Chen

Books Beyond Boundaries

ROYAL COLLINS

The New Quantum Mechanics

Kevin Chen

First published in 2024 by Royal Collins Publishing Group Inc.
Groupe Publication Royal Collins Inc.
550-555 boul. René-Lévesque O Montréal (Québec)
H2Z1B1 Canada

10 9 8 7 6 5 4 3 2 1

ISBN: 978-1-4878-1178-5

To find out more about our publications,
please visit www.royalcollins.com.

Part 1

Discovering the Quantum World

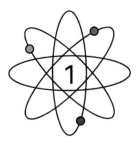

THE MYSTERIOUS MICROCOSM

1.1 Classical Mechanics

At the end of the seventeenth century, marked by the publication of Isaac Newton's *Principia Mathematica*, humanity entered the era of classical mechanics. This field's extensive accomplishments are evident in its application across scientific research and production technologies. Since Newton's groundbreaking work, classical mechanics has been instrumental in driving significant advancements, including the First and Second Industrial Revolutions, substantially boosting productivity. Even today, Newton's principles guide diverse aspects of human life, from Mars rover landings to the trajectory of bullets. His influence post-seventeenth century significantly hastened technological revolutions.

However, as Friedrich Engels observed, "The world is not an ensemble of finished things; it is an ensemble of processes." Development is a journey, not an overnight achievement. This was true for classical mechanics, which evolved over time, especially after its initial foundations were established.

1.1.1 Religion Governing Science?

In early societies, limited by low productivity and creativity, humans struggled to understand many natural phenomena. Consequently, they instinctively believed in mysterious or divine forces beyond their understanding. This belief system led to the birth of religion and theology, which played central roles in explaining the world, spreading beliefs, providing comfort, and delivering justice. Religion permeated political, economic, and cultural spheres. In ancient Greece, rulers elevated religion above other cultural aspects, granting it absolute dominance over science, philosophy, and other cultural forms.

Early science, primarily based on nature and life experiences and artifact creation, was overshadowed by religion. Ancient Greek philosophers and scientists like Aristotle and Ptolemy, who merged philosophy with natural sciences, attempted to explain natural phenomena within the constraints of contemporary technology.

Aristotle's theories on force and motion are notable examples. He proposed that heavier objects fall faster than lighter ones and that force is necessary to maintain an object's motion. Although these theories were later disproven, they influenced scientific thinking for centuries.

Ptolemy, another prominent ancient Greek figure, was a mathematician and astronomer. His geocentric theory, further developed by Aristotle, shaped views on Earth, the sun, the moon, and stars for an extended period. This model posited a finite universe with Earth at its center. According to geocentrism, the universe consists of nine concentric celestial spheres, with the Earth at the quiet center. While such ideas seem outdated now, they represented the pinnacle of human understanding of the cosmos at the time.

Aristotle's and Ptolemy's theories, which satisfactorily explained everyday phenomena and planetary movement, were long revered as classics. Christianity integrated Aristotle's concepts with its doctrine, asserting God as the prime mover, thus cementing these ideas in people's minds for over a millennium. Ptolemy's geocentrism, backed by the Catholic Church, became the dominant thought paradigm.

1.1.2 Emerging from the Geocentric Era

For over a millennium, the geocentric theory dominated human understanding. However, amid the burgeoning commodity economy and the rise of early capitalists like bankers and wealthy merchants in fourteenth-century Italy, a movement for intellectual liberation began. Advocating for human freedom, these early capitalists opposed the Church's and feudalism's constraints on thought. They yearned for a revival of the cultures of ancient Greece and Rome obliterated during the Middle Ages. This movement, known as the Renaissance in Europe, took humanism as its core, emphasizing human-centeredness over God-centeredness and opposing religious superstitions to free the mind.

This cultural shift catalyzed unprecedented scientific development. As astronomical observations became more accurate, Ptolemy's geocentric theory increasingly failed to explain celestial phenomena. Scholars began questioning and revising the geocentric model, leading to its growing complexity. It was Nicolaus Copernicus who steered humanity from geocentric to heliocentric thinking. In 1491, Copernicus, studying at the University of Cracow, meticulously analyzed Ptolemy's doctrines and identified numerous inaccuracies. He believed that for astronomy to advance, developing a new cosmic structure system was crucial rather than continually revising the geocentric model.

Embracing the Pythagorean view of the universe as harmonious and governed by simple mathematical relations, Copernicus revered the sun as the universe's center. His continuous observations and calculations convinced him that Earth and other planets revolve around the sun. In 1516, Copernicus published *On the Revolutions of the Heavenly Spheres*, rigorously arguing for the motion of the planets and positing three patterns of motion in the solar system: Earth's annual revolution around the sun, its daily rotation on its axis (explaining day and night), and its axial tilt (accounting for seasonal changes).

Regrettably, Copernicus's heliocentric theory faced significant opposition from the Church, and the publication of his work encountered numerous challenges. The Italian thinker Giordano Bruno (1548–1600), who advocated heliocentrism and opposed geocentrism, was condemned as a "heretic" by the Church and was executed in Rome's Piazza delle Flore in 1600.

Despite these challenges, the scientific quest for understanding persisted. Decades after Copernicus, Johannes Kepler built upon his heliocentrism with the groundbreaking Kepler's Laws of Planetary Motion. Born in 1571 in Württemberg, Germany, Kepler enrolled at the University of Tübingen at age sixteen to study literature. His astronomy professor, Maestlin, secretly taught heliocentrism, deeply influencing Kepler and sparking his interest in astronomy and mathematics. In 1596, Kepler published his first astronomical work, *Mysterium Cosmographicum*, affirming the Copernican doctrine. Despite inaccuracies in his conclusions, Kepler's mathematical talent was recognized by Danish astronomer Tycho Brahe.

However, Brahe did not support the heliocentric theory. In 1600, Kepler accepted Brahe's invitation to work as his assistant at an observatory outside Prague. Brahe's astronomical data were remarkably accurate. After working with Brahe for over a year and inheriting his extensive observational data following Brahe's death, Kepler became his successor. Kepler meticulously analyzed Brahe's observations to validate the correct theory.

In 1609, Kepler published *Astronomia Nova*, formalizing two fundamental laws of planetary motion: the law of orbits (planets move around the sun in elliptical paths, with the sun at one focus of the ellipse) and the law of areas (planets move fastest at perihelion and slowest at aphelion, with lines connecting planets to the sun covering equal areas in equal times). Later, Kepler introduced the third law—the law of periods, stating that the cube of a planet's orbital semi-major axis is proportional to the square of its orbital period. These laws, known as "Kepler's Laws of Planetary Motion," refined the Copernican system, dismissed orthogonal orbits, and overthrew the Ptolemaic geocentric theory, simplifying the universe's complex structure and making it more comprehensible. Kepler's work transformed astronomy into a precise discipline.

Meanwhile, Galileo Galilei brought new scientific perspectives through experimental and methodological innovations. Known for discoveries such as the time-equivalence of pendulum swings, the design of the thermometer (ushering in the field of thermodynamics), and the development of the telescope (initiating the era of telescopic observation of the universe), Galileo is celebrated as a pivotal figure in the history of physics.

Most notably, Galileo challenged the long-standing notions about force and motion, proposing for the first time that force is not the cause of an object's motion and introducing the concept of inertia—though his theory of circular inertia was later rejected. In his *Dialogue Concerning the Two Chief World Systems*, Galileo employed a dialogue style to make his ideas more accessible. He introduced the concept of acceleration to clarify the relationship between force and motion, laying the foundation for quantitative calculations in physics. Galileo also emphasized that "experimentation is the foundation of theoretical research," elevating the status of physical experiments. He is often hailed as the father of modern physics.

1.1.3 The Apple That Revolutionized Classical Thought

While scientists like Kepler and Galileo laid the groundwork for modern physics with theories and experiments, their theories still needed to be completed. For instance, Kepler proposed the laws of planetary motion but did not explain why planets revolve around the sun. Completing the physics edifice required a pivotal figure to synthesize and refine these scientific theories. That key figure was Isaac Newton, a renowned scientist whose work continues to influence us today.

In 1688, Newton published *The Mathematical Principles of Natural Philosophy*, propelling humanity into the age of classical physics. This work compiled Newton's significant achievements, notably in studying gravity and formulating the three laws of mechanics.

Newton posited that the Earth exerts a force on objects on its surface, conforming to the "law of gravity," and thereby proved and perfected Kepler's laws of celestial motion. The story of Newton's discovery of gravity, often associated with an apple, is well-known. This seemingly simple realization that all objects exert mutual attraction was a monumental discovery. While Kepler and others had some understanding of celestial motion and theoretical generalization, Newton's theory was more systematic, comprehensive, and capable of explaining many natural phenomena.

Newton's Law of Universal Gravitation states that any two mass points exert a mutual attraction. The direction of this gravitational force aligns with the line connecting the centers of the two mass points, and its magnitude is directly proportional to the product of their masses and inversely proportional to the square of the distance between them. This law was crucial in unraveling the universe's mysteries and understanding the planets' motion around stars and satellites around planets.

Newton also specialized in formulating his three laws of mechanics—laws of inertia, acceleration, and action-reaction.

Before Newton, it was assumed that continuous force was necessary for an object's motion, similar to propelling a power-lost automobile, and that an object would stop without force, as per Aristotle's view, where lighter objects fall slower than heavier ones. Newton's view differed radically. He believed that an object at rest or in uniform linear motion remains so unless acted upon by an external force. This principle, Newton's law of inertia, challenged the old notion that force was necessary to maintain motion.

Acceleration, the change in an object's motion speed, can either increase or decrease (the latter is considered negative acceleration). The cause of an object's acceleration is force, necessary for changing an object's state from motion to rest or vice versa or altering the speed of a moving object.

Regarding action and reaction forces, these are intuitively understood. For example, if a monkey shakes a stone column, the monkey produces the action force, and the column generates a reaction force. The relationship between these forces is threefold: they are equal in magnitude, opposite in direction, and act along the same line. This understanding forms Newton's third law of mechanics.

Newton attributed all physical movement and deformation to "force." In the absence of force, objects maintain their state of motion; with force, objects move or deform. The greater the force, the more significant the movement. Newton's principles scientifically explain many common life phenomena, such as why passengers lean forward when a car moves or the Earth revolves around the sun.

With Newton's contributions, the structure of classical mechanics was finally complete. However, just as scientists relished the clarity brought by modern physics, two dark clouds loomed on the horizon, signaling new challenges and discoveries to come.

1.2   Dark Clouds in a Clear Sky

Two periods stand out among the greatest eras in the history of physics: the late seventeenth and early twentieth centuries. At the end of the seventeenth century, Isaac Newton synthesized the empirical theories of his predecessors with great success in *The Mathematical Principles of Natural Philosophy*, ushering in the era of classical physics.

By the early twentieth century, scientists generally believed that Newton's classical mechanics, Maxwell's classical electromagnetic field theory, and other classical physics theories could explain all discovered physical phenomena. This belief led many physicists to think that the "edifice of physics has been completed," requiring only minor subsequent revisions. However, at this time, dark clouds began to drift in from the far side of the classical physics edifice.

1.2.1 The "Ultraviolet Catastrophe" of Classical Mechanics

Although classical physics seemed complete, it soon faced new challenges. As science progressed and the world changed, Newtonian mechanics began to fail in certain special scenarios. One notable issue, referred to as one of the "two dark clouds" by Lord Kelvin, a renowned physicist and former president of the Royal Society, in a 1900 lecture, pertained to the ultraviolet catastrophe and the problem of blackbody radiation.

Before 1900, light was considered a wave, possessing a certain frequency—the number of vibrations a body makes in a unit of time. For instance, a bouncing basketball at one bounce per second is said to have a frequency of 1 hertz. Similarly, the frequency of light waves, measured in hertz, corresponds to the number of vibrations per second at a point. The energy carried by light waves depends on this frequency: the more vibrations per second, the greater the energy.

It was common knowledge that any solid or liquid emits electromagnetic waves, or light, at any temperature. For example, a heating block of iron first emits invisible infrared radiation, changing the electromagnetic waves it emits. As its temperature rises above 550 degrees, it begins to emit visible red light, transitioning through orange, yellow-white, and eventually bluish-white as it gets hotter. According to the principle of the three primary colors, simultaneous emission of these colors results in white light. For instance, at 2,200 degrees, the tungsten filament in an incandescent light bulb emits white light. Heated beyond 5,000 degrees, an object emits higher frequency light like blue, violet, and ultraviolet light.

Before 1900, it was believed that a heated object emitted electromagnetic waves equally across all frequencies, implying that higher temperatures would result in higher energy emissions and extremely high-frequency electromagnetic waves at temperatures of 100,000 degrees. This logic led to the hypothesis that the frequency of light emitted by a continuously heated object would be infinite, resulting in infinite total radiation—a scenario Paul Ehrenfest labeled the "ultraviolet catastrophe" in 1911. This theoretical result, contradicting reality, suggested that high-temperature objects do not emit infinite amounts of high-frequency light.

In studying electromagnetic waves, scientists developed an ideal model known as a blackbody for examining thermal radiation laws independent of material properties. A blackbody, a standard object in radiation studies, absorbs all incoming electromagnetic radiation without reflection or transmission. Thus, it has an absorption coefficient of 1 and a transmission coefficient of 0 for all wavelengths of electromagnetic waves. All objects above absolute zero emit thermal radiation, with higher temperatures resulting in greater total energy and a higher proportion of short-wavelength components.

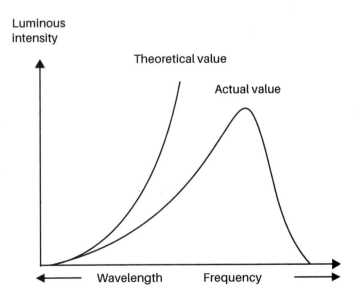

Physicists measuring actual radiation emitted by blackbodies found that contrary to classical theory predictions, blackbody radiation does not tend toward infinity in the ultraviolet region but peaks near the middle of the visible light spectrum, then decreases with shorter wavelengths. For example, the sun, an excellent blackbody, emits most of its radiation as visible light, not ultraviolet, despite its surface temperature of 6,000 degrees.

This discrepancy between theoretical predictions and empirical measurements regarding light as a wave left physicists puzzled and unable to reconcile the anomaly.

The challenges posed by the ultraviolet catastrophe and blackbody radiation marked inexplicable failures in classical physics, shaking its foundations and paving the way for new scientific discoveries and theories.

1.2.2 The Limitations of Classical Mechanics in Physics

Although seemingly comprehensive, classical physics encountered phenomena it couldn't explain, revealing many limitations. Classical mechanics, derived from everyday macroscopic mechanical movements, failed to describe the behavior of microscopic particles, such as electrons, protons, and neutrons, discovered toward the end of the 19th and the beginning of the 20th centuries. These particles, exhibiting both particle and wave-like properties, couldn't be adequately explained by classical mechanics.

For instance, in 1898, Marie and Pierre Curie discovered the radioactive elements polonium and radium, indicating that atoms were not the smallest units of matter but had complex structures. In 1911, the British physicist Ernest Rutherford, based on his alpha particle scattering experiment, proposed the famous atomic model. In this model, an atom's positive charge and mass were concentrated in a small central nucleus, around which electrons orbited. However, this model raised a question: Why didn't the negatively charged electrons fall into the positively charged nucleus? According to classical electrodynamics, an electron orbiting a nucleus should radiate energy and eventually spiral into the nucleus, leading to a "collapse." Yet, atoms are stably existing in the real world, a fact classical physics couldn't explain.

Classical physics also couldn't account for the photoelectric effect. Simply put, this effect involves the emission of electrons from a metal surface when illuminated by light. This phenomenon is peculiar because whether electrons are ejected from the same metal surface depends not on the light's intensity but on its frequency, clearly contradicting classical physics wave theory.

Furthermore, the existence of atomic spectra, the specific heat of solids, and atomic stability further highlighted the limitations of classical physics. People gradually realized the need for more classical mechanics, which viewed time and space as absolutes in the Newtonian framework, clearly distinguishing between high-speed and low-speed motion and between the microscopic and macroscopic worlds.

To dispel the dark clouds looming over the edifice of classical physics and explain these unexplained phenomena, physicists inadvertently opened the doors to the quantum world. At the dawn of the 20th century, they began to explore the invisible and silent world of atoms, atomic nuclei, and fundamental particles. A new realm emerged through theoretical and experimental investigations—the kingdom of quantum physics.

Compared to the era of classical physics, the quantum era, almost three hundred years later, was filled with mystery and splendor. The advent of relativity and quantum theory created a new kingdom in the world of physics and completely overturned and rebuilt the entire physics framework. These theories continue to exert a profound influence today.

1.3 From Planck's Formula to the Photoelectric Effect

The problems exposed by classical physics drew physicists to further exploration. In addressing the issue of blackbody radiation arising from the "ultraviolet catastrophe," Max Planck innovatively proposed the quantum hypothesis. He assumed that the energy of light radiated by oscillating electrons was quantized, leading to an expression that matched experimental results remarkably well. Although Planck initially doubted his own theory, even considering it absurd, as he later stated, "Quantization was merely an act of desperation." However, Planck eventually opened the door to the quantum world, leading humanity from the classical physics era to another equally splendid era—the Quantum Age.

1.3.1 Planck: A Desperate Measure

Before Planck proposed the quantum hypothesis, there were two main theories of blackbody radiation. One was Wilhelm Wien's formula. In 1893, the German physicist Wien discovered that the frequency at which radiation energy is maximal is proportional to the absolute temperature of the blackbody, and he provided a formula for the distribution of radiation energy over frequency. Wien believed that since the discussion of blackbody radiation concerns the emission of electromagnetic waves, and it is known in electrodynamics that charged particles or currents emit electromagnetic waves when they oscillate, the blackbody radiation problem should be solvable based on electrodynamics. Wien's formula reflected the discrete characteristics of objects, but it only conformed to experimental data in the short wavelength range, failing at longer wavelengths.

The other theory was the Rayleigh-Jeans formula. In 1899, the British physicists Lord Rayleigh and James Hopwood Jeans derived another formula for the distribution of radiation energy over frequency based on electrodynamics and statistical physics. In this formula, the radiated energy diverges as the frequency approaches infinity, reflecting the continuity of energy. However, while the Rayleigh-Jeans formula matched experimental data in the long wavelength range, remedying the deficiencies of Wien's formula, it lost the advantages of Wien's formula in the short wavelength range.

To resolve these issues, Planck interpolated between Wien's and Rayleigh-Jeans' formulas, resulting in a formula that perfectly matched experimental results—the famous Planck formula. At the end of 1900, Planck proposed an interpretation for his formula—on December 14, he presented his bold hypothesis to the German Physical Society in a paper titled "On the Theory of the Energy Distribution Law of the Normal Spectrum," stating that the energy of oscillators is not continuously variable, but can only take multiples of a minimum value, which is proportional to the oscillator's frequency. This minimum value, derived from fitting experimental data, was termed the "Planck constant." This assumption led to the Planck formula.

Since the energy of electromagnetic oscillators that absorb or emit electromagnetic waves must be consistent with their frequency, the idea that the energy of these oscillators can only take discrete values led to the notion that blackbody radiation and absorption of energy, are also quantized, termed "energy quanta." Simply put, the electromagnetic waves radiated from a blackbody are not emitted continuously but in discrete packets, each referred to by Planck as a "quantum." Thus, the preliminary concept of quantum mechanics was first proposed, and Planck successfully ushered humanity into the realm of quantum mechanics. December 14 was later known as "Quantum Day." As the founder of quantum mechanics, Planck was awarded the Nobel Prize in Physics in 1918, and Asteroid 1069 was named after him.

Planck's concept of energy quanta broke the fundamental assumption of classical physics that physical quantities could take continuous values, proposing the idea of discrete energy for the first time. This negated the law of equipartition of energy and ran counter to classical physics. Even Planck himself had reservations, cautioning in his paper, "I present this cautiously, not to be taken too seriously." Indeed, the physics community of the time did not take his theory seriously. Even five years after Planck proposed his formula, attempts were still being made to explain blackbody radiation from a classical physics standpoint.

1.3.2 Einstein: Quantizing Photons

Planck's introduction of quantum mechanics was just the beginning, and he couldn't provide more physical explanations for this quantum hypothesis. He believed it was a mathematical derivation, allowing theory and empirical data to align across the spectrum. Soon after, Albert Einstein refined and advanced Planck's quantum theory.

Building on Planck's idea that energy is not continuous but quantized, with each quantum related to frequency, Einstein hypothesized that light, being a form of electromagnetic wave and thus energy, might also be discontinuous. In 1905, Einstein published the paper "A Heuristic Point of View Concerning the Production and Transformation of Light," formally proposing his hypothesis. In this paper, Einstein boldly assumed that light consists of discontinuous "energy quanta," or "photons." He suggested that photons are massless at rest but acquire mass in motion. However, Einstein's concept of "photons" differed from Newton's "corpuscular" theory of light, where Newton considered light as solid "particles," while Einstein's photons were quantized.

Einstein's further research revealed that when photons hit a metal plate, the electrons in the metal absorb the photons' energy. If this process absorbs excessive energy beyond what atomic nuclei can bind, the electrons break free, reaching the metal's surface. This phenomenon is known as the "photoelectric effect." Einstein's explanation clarified why the energy of photoelectrons relates only to frequency, not light intensity. Even with weak light intensity, if the frequency is high enough, it can produce high-energy photons that cause bound electrons to escape. Conversely, intense light of low frequency cannot release any high-energy photons to free the electrons.

Einstein was awarded the Nobel Prize in Physics in 1921 for his discovery of the photoelectric effect. His work significantly advanced our understanding of light.

Over the next decade, Einstein continued his research on light, laying an essential foundation for the invention of lasers. Our modern life has been dramatically altered by continuous research on light. For instance, the Internet is built on communication devices like optical fibers, whose applications stem from photonics research.

Consider the growing need for renewable energy sources as fossil fuels deplete. Solar energy, a clean, renewable source, hinges on ample sunlight. In this process, the role of photons is crucial. The sun, the source of all energy on Earth, is found to derive its power from constant fusion reactions (nuclear fusion) occurring within. Thus, research on replicating this super-technology on Earth began. If successful, it could completely resolve humanity's energy issues. One key method involves using high-power lasers to achieve this.

Lasers also excel in medical fields, like the common use of laser eye surgery to correct myopia. Additionally, lasers are applied in various lighting, distance measurement, and building alignment tasks.

Our understanding of light has not only brought immense convenience to life but also plays a significant role in modern physics. The new issues raised by the photoelectric effect have influenced the entire scope of modern physics research, such as the study of emerging quantum materials and superconductors. At the cutting edge of physics, the photoelectric effect remains irreplaceable.

Whether it was Planck's introduction of the quantum hypothesis or Einstein's development of it, these theories have laid a crucial foundation for scientists to understand quantum theory. Their contributions have been immensely significant to physics and, indeed, to all of human society.

1.4 What Are Quanta, and Why Mechanics?

1.4.1 Are Quanta Not Particles?

Though Planck and Einstein led humanity into the world of quanta, the question remains: What exactly are quanta? Before delving into quanta, let's first explore the material world. Historically, the quest to understand the composition of matter has been ongoing. An ancient saying from *Zhuangzi* goes, "A one-foot stick, halved each day, will never be exhausted," implying that matter can be infinitely divided without ever being depleted.

What, then, constitutes the most fundamental unit of our world? Through generations of scientific exploration, scientists have discovered the smallest observable entities to date—elementary particles. Modern physics, particularly the Standard Model, identifies 62 types of elementary particles as the universe's building blocks.

The journey to this discovery has been winding. At the beginning of the last century, breakthroughs in physics ushered in the atomic era. Scientists found that atoms contain nuclei surrounded by electrons, with the nucleus itself being exceedingly small. For instance, a hydrogen atom has a radius of about 5.3×10^{-11} m (0.053 nm), while its nucleus is approximately 8.8×10^{-16} m (0.88 fm) in radius. If a hydrogen atom were the size of Earth, with a radius of 6,400 km, its nucleus would be only about 107 m in diameter, roughly the height of a 35-story building. Yet even such minute atomic nuclei can be further divided.

The constituents of atomic nuclei come in various types. Initially, scientists discovered photons, electrons, protons, and neutrons, later identifying positrons, neutrinos, quarks, leptons, mesons, and more as elementary particles. These particles, minuscule in the macroscopic world, vary in size. Protons and neutrons are relatively larger, with about one ten-billionth of a centimeter diameters. Other elementary particles, like neutrinos, are even smaller.

These particles, though tiny, possess mass. Photons are unique, having zero rest mass. A 40-watt bulb emits trillions of photons per second. The heaviest particle, a top quark, weighs 340 times more than a proton but exists for only a billionth of a second.

Elementary particles exhibit intriguing phenomena, such as transmuting into each other. For example, when an electron and a positron collide, they transform into photons. Protons and antiprotons can convert into antineutrons and vice versa.

Modern physics describes these phenomena as "symmetry." If a particle exists, its antiparticle also exists. When matter and antimatter particles meet, they annihilate, transforming into energy-rich photons. Conversely, high-energy particle collisions can generate new matter-antimatter pairs, showing that matter and energy are interchangeable.

Moreover, advancements in science and technology have revealed that even elementary particles like quarks make up protons and neutrons. Modern electron microscopes cannot directly observe quarks; their existence is inferred through experiments.

Currently, six types of quarks are known: up, down, charm, strange, top, and bottom. Quarks represent the smallest entities identified in physics, raising questions about whether they can be further divided and whether even more fundamental entities exist within quarks.

Quanta exists in this microscopic world. In the early era of quantum mechanics, just after Planck introduced the concept of quanta, they often represented a physical quantity. Quanta was understood as indivisible basic units—reflecting the Latin origin of the word "quantum," meaning "how much."

It's important to note that "quanta" does not refer to an actual particle like atoms, electrons, or protons. Instead, it's an abstract concept, given specific meaning only when combined with particular nouns, such as "photon" or "light quantum," referring to the basic unit of light.

Imagine climbing a mountain: continuous ascent is like walking up a gentle slope, where each step can vary in length. Discontinuous ascent, however, is like climbing stairs, where each step must be a whole number multiple of a stair. Each stair represents an indivisible basic unit.

Since Planck's time, many physics luminaries have continually refined quantum theory. In the first half of the twentieth century—a period of vigorous development in physics—researchers like Einstein, Schrödinger, Dirac, and Heisenberg gradually established a comprehensive quantum theory, ushering quantum mechanics into a new era.

In this new era of quantum mechanics, "quantum" often signifies a property, such as uncertainty, wave-particle duality, or superposition, encompassing quantum effects. It's also directly understood as wave-particle duality, a fundamental characteristic of the quantum world. The wave-particle duality concept, proposed by Louis de Broglie in 1924 based on Einstein's "light quantum" hypothesis, posited that particles like electrons can also be waves. Thus, all matter exhibits wave-particle duality.

Unlike Newtonian mechanics, which describes the macroscopic world, quantum theory is used to depict microscopic particles, finally enabling humanity to comprehend the world we inhabit fully.

1.4.2 Mechanics in the Quantum World

While quanta are a fundamental aspect of the quantum world, so is mechanics. Mechanics is the science that studies the laws of the mechanical motion of matter. Classical mechanics, however, is focused on the phenomena and laws of mechanical motion of macroscopic objects at low speeds—"macroscopic" compared to microscopic particles like atoms and "low speed" relative to the speed of light. Mechanical motion is the change in an object's spatial position over time. The mechanical motions directly observed and initially studied in everyday life are predominantly macroscopic and low speed.

Since ancient times, people have conducted astronomical observations due to the agricultural need to determine seasons. In the late 16th century, Galileo's telescope allowed detailed and precise observations of the planets orbiting the sun. In the 17th century, Kepler formulated three empirical laws of planetary motion around the sun, drawing from these observations. Around the same period, Galileo conducted experiments on falling bodies and projectiles, proposing preliminary mechanical motion theories. Newton delved deeper into these empirical laws and preliminary theories, discovering the fundamental laws of macroscopic low-speed mechanical motion and laying the foundation for classical mechanics.

However, unlike classical mechanics, the mechanics of the quantum world mainly represent a type of motion of objects rather than a tangible force. While it does involve strong, weak, and electromagnetic forces, quantum mechanics is named more to differentiate from the traditional modes of motion in classical mechanics. Disciplines termed mechanics typically involve strict mathematical equations and highly precise study content.

Quantum mechanics, despite being a mysterious and profound science, is indeed a theory developed from objective phenomena with high experimental precision and theoretical accuracy. It can even be considered one of the most precise theories among all scientific disciplines. Take, for example, Richard Feynman's illustration regarding the electron's anomalous magnetic moment. The discrepancy between the purely theoretical calculation in quantum electrodynamics and actual experimental measurements is as minute as the thickness of a hair over the distance from New York to Los Angeles. This precision underscores the accuracy of quantum mechanics as a theory. Moreover, many Nobel Prizes in Physics, including recent ones, have been awarded for research related to quantum mechanics. Some say quantum mechanics is the pinnacle of human intellectual achievement to date.

With this, we can form a preliminary impression of quantum mechanics: it's mysterious and disruptive, yet scientific and precise. It's a study of contradictions that still follows a certain logic. Perhaps these peculiarities are what make quantum mechanics so attractive to physicists, continually inspiring their dedication and research.

Part 2

Inquiring into Quantum Mechanics

FROM DISARRAY TO REBIRTH

2.1 Venturing into the Atomic World

Despite Planck's quantum hypothesis successfully ushering us into the world of quanta, as Niels Bohr, a foundational figure in quantum physics, said: "Anyone who is not shocked by quantum mechanics has not understood it." For physicists of the time, the quantum world remained mysterious and unfamiliar. In the first ten years following the inception of quantum mechanics, a period of bewilderment ensued. Understanding microscopic particles from a microscopic perspective was the initial challenge in developing quantum mechanics.

2.1.1 Rutherford: From Smashing Potatoes to Smashing Atoms

We now know that all matter is composed of molecules and atoms, with molecules being combinations of two or more atoms. The secret of matter's properties lies within molecules and atoms. An atom's radius is typically on the order of one ten-billionth of a centimeter, vastly larger than the cells visible under an optical microscope. Exploring the internal structure of molecules and atoms allows us to enter the microscopic world. One significant figure who led us into this realm was Ernest Rutherford.

Rutherford, a New Zealander, was digging potatoes in a field when he received his acceptance letter from Cambridge University. This young man, once a potato digger, later uncovered the great secrets of atoms in the microscopic world.

Rutherford's primary research was an extension of Henri Becquerel's work on radioactivity. In March 1896, Becquerel discovered that photographic plates were exposed and stored alongside potassium uranyl sulfate but wrapped in black paper. He surmised that this was due to some unknown radiation emitted by the uranium salt. By May of the same year, he confirmed the existence of natural radioactivity through experiments with pure uranium metal. However, even Becquerel needed to understand this emitted radiation's nature fully.

Building on this foundation and using magnetic fields, Rutherford discovered that naturally radioactive substances emit two types of rays: one bending upward and the other downward, indicating different electrical properties. The positively charged particles were named alpha particles, and the negatively charged ones were called beta particles. Rutherford won the Nobel Prize in Physics in 1908 for this discovery. However, his most significant work was the discovery of the atomic nucleus and the proton.

Regarding discovering the atomic nucleus, Rutherford is often called the "father of nuclear physics." He said, "I used to smash potatoes as a young man; as I grew older, I smashed atoms."

The specific process goes back to after Rutherford separates alpha particles. In 1909, he conducted the most important experiment of his life. He decided to bombard a gold foil with alpha particles. To his surprise, most alpha particles passed straight through without even a slight deflection, but a few were deflected back.

According to his teacher J.J. Thomson's atomic model, the positive charge in an atom is evenly distributed, and since electrons are much lighter than alpha particles, positively charged alpha particles should pass through atoms with minimal obstruction, at most undergoing small-angle scattering. So, how to explain the large angle scattering of alpha particles in Rutherford's experiment? After thorough analysis and reflection, Rutherford boldly overturned Thomson's atomic model and established his own.

Rutherford postulated that most alpha particles passed straight through due to vast empty spaces inside the atom; the few deflected back did so because of a small, hard core within the atom. He envisioned a model with a tiny, positively charged atomic nucleus surrounded by many negatively charged electrons. The electrons did not adhere to the nucleus but orbited it in fixed paths, similar to planets orbiting the sun, leading to the planetary model.

According to Rutherford's model, most alpha particles would pass through the large empty spaces within an atom. Even if they hit an electron, the alpha particles, being over 7,000 times heavier, would knock electrons aside without affecting their own trajectory. Only when an alpha particle comes very close to the atomic nucleus would it be deflected back due to the strong repulsion between the two positively charged particles and the much larger mass of the nucleus.

Rutherford's work allowed humanity to recognize a new microscopic world. Further exploration based on Rutherford's atomic model has enabled us to glimpse a world entirely different from the macroscopic one. In the microscopic world of atoms, an atom consists of a nucleus and surrounding electrons, with the nucleus's radius being only about one ten-thousandth of the atom's. In other words, if an atom were the size of a residential area, the nucleus would not even be as big as a grape. This reveals the vast emptiness within an atom. Additionally, the atomic nucleus is composed of protons and neutrons, each of which is made up of three fundamental particles called quarks.

In essence, the microscopic world is almost empty. In our sensory world, we can physically touch each object with a definite surface, size, and location. However, from an atomic perspective, everything is blurred. The shapes and colors of objects we see result from the selective reflection of different frequency photons by the object's atoms.

2.1.2 Bohr: Stabilizing the Unstable Atomic Nucleus

Although Rutherford proposed a novel atomic model, it had theoretical limitations—Rutherford did not clarify how electrons were distributed within the atom. According to his model, an electron in circular motion would generate an alternating electromagnetic field, continuously emitting electromagnetic waves and thereby losing energy. This energy loss would draw the electron closer to the nucleus, ultimately causing a collision. Thus, based on Rutherford's model, atoms should be unstable.

Addressing the unresolved issues of Rutherford's model, another key figure in the development of quantum mechanics emerged: Niels Bohr.

Born in Copenhagen, Denmark, in 1885, Bohr was an outstanding student, especially in the sciences. At 26, having just completed his doctorate, Bohr, with his excellent academic record, joined Rutherford's laboratory at Cambridge University.

In 1911, when Bohr arrived, Rutherford introduced his atomic model, gaining widespread acclaim and embarking on a lecture tour. Bohr attended one of Rutherford's lectures and afterward approached him to learn more, earning

Rutherford's approval. Consequently, Rutherford took Bohr to the University of Manchester as a professor. Their first task was to investigate why the atomic nucleus could be stable. According to classical electromagnetism, continuously moving electrons would emit electromagnetic waves, leading to atomic collapse. However, atoms were not observed to collapse, posing a challenge for Bohr.

At 26, Bohr first questioned the Rutherford model itself, recalling Planck and Einstein's quantum hypotheses. Bohr proposed that electron orbits were not singular but numerous and discrete. He termed these "stationary orbits," suggesting that electrons could only occupy these specific paths. To simplify, it's like a staircase where a person can only stand on a step, not between them because the orbits are quantized. If an electron moves from one orbit to another, it does so instantaneously, akin to teleporting.

In Bohr's model, the quantization of electron orbits meant that physical quantities like radii and energy also became quantized. For example, since orbits could only take specific values, their radii were also fixed. Likewise, energy levels on each orbit were discrete, with no gradual transitions.

Bohr's bold and radical hypothesis successfully addressed the stability of atoms. As previously mentioned, moving electrons would emit electromagnetic waves, causing instability. However, according to Bohr, electrons on discrete orbits do not emit waves, only during transitions between orbits.

Bohr also believed there was no clear boundary between the macroscopic and microscopic worlds. As orbits extend outward, they become part of macroscopic issues, losing quantum effects. He later termed this the complementarity principle.

Bohr then attempted to translate his ideas into formulas, deriving energy levels for each orbit. After four months, he presented a complete set of formulas to Rutherford, who did not initially accept his theory.

This was understandable, as Rutherford had tasked Bohr with investigating atomic stability, not developing a new atomic model. Bohr's explanation of atomic stability seemed far-fetched at the time. Rutherford initially refused to publish Bohr's findings. Since publication required the adviser's approval, Bohr's work remained unpublished, and he returned home to marry.

However, as events unfolded, Bohr's return home proved fortuitous. He later met his university colleague Hans, a spectroscopy researcher, who introduced him to the Balmer formula. The similarity between Bohr's energy level formulas and the Balmer formula inspired him to write to Rutherford.

This time, Rutherford grasped the concept and quickly endorsed the publication of Bohr's paper in one of Britain's most authoritative journals. Bohr's paper, unsurprisingly, became epoch-making.

Bohr's work built upon previous research, positing that energy absorbed and released by electrons in atoms exists in discrete quanta. Correspondingly, the possible potential energy positions of electrons within atoms must also be discrete. These positions, known as energy levels, define electron transitions. Since electrons cannot exist outside these energy levels, they cannot fall into the nucleus and cause catastrophic annihilation. Bohr's theory successfully salvaged the nuclear model of the atom and introduced the concept of discreteness to subatomic realms. This marked the first explanation of spectral lines, elevating Bohr to the ranks of the 20th century's greatest physicists alongside Einstein.

2.1.3 The Misdirection of Early Quantum Theory

From Planck's blackbody radiation formula to Einstein's hypothesis of photons in his study of the photoelectric effect and Bohr's quantum theory of the hydrogen atom based on his analysis of atomic spectra, quantum science was continuously evolving. Shortly after Bohr presented his theory of the hydrogen atom, Sommerfeld extended Bohr's theory. He suggested that any physical system could exist in discrete "stationary states" and provided more general "quantization" rules.

Using this expanded theory, Sommerfeld discovered that electrons in an atom should have three quantum numbers instead of one, as in Bohr's theory. His quantum theory could explain more atomic-related phenomena, such as the Zeeman and Stark effects, which are complementary phenomena. The Zeeman effect involves the splitting of atomic (or molecular) spectral lines by an external magnetic field, while the Stark effect is the splitting caused by an external electric field.

However, theories like Planck's blackbody radiation formula, Einstein's photoelectric effect, or Bohr's atomic model were still early quantum theories or old quantum theories. The reason is that, while these theories opened the door to the quantum world, they were merely a mixture of classical theory and quantum conditions, making it difficult to explain the microscopic particle motion fully.

In fact, over these two decades, physicists made very limited progress, with discussions almost entirely centered around the "quantum nature" of energy: radiation energy comes in discrete quantities; electrons can only exist in certain discrete energy levels. Einstein's theory of light particles was an exception, the starting point for what is now known as wave-particle duality, but at the time, no one further developed or promoted Einstein's idea.

Looking back, the quantum theory of this period was full of limitations, riddled with flaws and gaps: Planck's derivation of the blackbody radiation formula was incorrect; Einstein's solid-state heat theory was obtained by analogy; Bohr almost cobbled together the energy levels of the hydrogen atom.

As Planck said, "Quantization was nothing more than a desperate move," and Bohr was also keenly aware of the inadequacies of his theory. His theory best described the hydrogen atom, but even for hydrogen, it could only predict the frequencies of spectral lines, not their intensities or the polarization of emitted photons.

To refine his theory, Bohr proposed a semi-intuitive correspondence principle, positing that the probability of electron transitions between energy levels could be described using classical Maxwell's equations. Combined with Einstein's theories of spontaneous and stimulated emission, Bohr successfully derived selection rules for transitions between energy levels. Dutch physicist Hendrik Anthony "Hans" Kramers (1894–1952) used this correspondence principle to further determine the intensity and polarization of all hydrogen atom spectral lines, aligning well with experimental results.

However, it soon became apparent that Bohr-Sommerfeld theory had many deficiencies and could not explain numerous experimental phenomena. For every success of the Bohr-Sommerfeld theory, there was a failure. It could not describe any atom or molecule with two or more electrons. For instance, it failed to produce the spectral lines of helium atoms and could not describe covalent bonds between molecules.

As one problem after another was exposed, scientists finally recognized that this newly born theory required fundamental changes, even altering basic assumptions. Thus, a revolution in quantum mechanics theory began to brew.

2.2 Quantum Mechanics: Out with the Old, In with the New

During the era of old quantum mechanics, Bohr took a decisive step. He made a radical assumption: electrons in an atom could only occupy discrete stationary states, including the ground state. Electrons transitioned between these states, altering their energy and emitting light of specific wavelengths depending on the energy difference between the states. Combining known laws with this peculiar hypothesis, Bohr cleared up the issue of atomic stability.

Although Bohr provided a quantitative description of the hydrogen atom's spectrum, his theory was fraught with contradictions, leading to repeated failures in developing Bohr's quantum theory. However, the concept of wave-particle duality unraveled the confusion of physicists during the old quantum era and heralded the emergence of new quantum mechanics. Today, wave-particle duality is considered a fundamental characteristic of the quantum world.

2.2.1 Wave-Particle Duality: The Fundamental Characteristic of the Quantum World

Traditionally, the properties of waves and particles were seen as incompatible in physics. Waves could occupy and interact across entire spaces, with different waves coexisting at the same location. Particles, however, imply the existence of an object at a specific location in space, excluding other particles.

This contradiction deeply misled physicists, who strictly approached microscopic particles from a particle perspective. While perfectly explaining some results, they faced the embarrassment of being overturned by new discoveries. Einstein first broke this deadlock, proposing the concept of photons in his explanation of the photoelectric effect and boldly predicting that light has both wave and particle properties.

Later, Robert Andrews Millikan's experiments confirmed Einstein's photoelectric effect. However, Maxwell's equations couldn't derive Einstein's non-classical statements. Under these circumstances, physicists were forced to acknowledge that light also possesses particle properties in addition to wave properties. From this point, the traditional concept of the incompatibility of waves and particles was shattered.

Inspired by Einstein's research, French physicist Louis de Broglie developed a bold idea: If, in studying light, only its wave properties were considered while ignoring its particle properties, could a similar mistake have been made in studying microscopic particles? Might their wave properties have been overlooked?

Based on Einstein's "light quantum" hypothesis, de Broglie extended the photon momentum and wavelength concept, formally proposing the "matter wave" hypothesis in late 1924. He suggested that if wave-like light can also be particle-like, particles, like electrons, can also be waves. Thus, like light, all matter possesses wave-particle duality. His daring hypothesis sent shockwaves through the academic world. Particles and waves, completely different material forms, seemed irreconcilable in classical physics. Yet Einstein admiringly commented: "A corner of the great veil has been lifted." De Broglie's hypothesis allowed subatomic particles to be partially described in terms of particles and waves.

In his doctoral thesis, de Broglie engaged in extensive quantitative discussions around this viewpoint. First, he posited that if a particle's momentum is p, its wavelength is λ = h/p. Second, he theorized that if an electron is a wave, it would form standing waves around the proton. Following this thought, de Broglie re-markably re-derived Bohr's orbits and energy levels for the hydrogen atom. Finally, de Broglie predicted that electrons would exhibit scattering and interference, a hypothesis proven in electron double-slit interference experiments. Subsequently, wave-particle duality was demonstrated for other microscopic particles, and de Broglie himself was awarded the Nobel Prize in Physics for this ingenious hypothesis.

2.2.2 Schrödinger Equation: A Key Step in Quantum Theory

The wave-particle duality proposed by de Broglie also inspired another renowned physicist, Erwin Schrödinger, with whom we are familiar today.

Schrödinger, born in Vienna, enjoyed a comfortable childhood thanks to his father's craftsmanship business and received a quality education in school. There, he found his interests and displayed potential as a philosophical scientist, endeavoring to demonstrate the connection between ancient Greek philosophy and the origins of European science. This passion for philosophy greatly aided Schrödinger's understanding of modern science, particularly quantum physics.

While studying at the University of Vienna, Schrödinger devoted himself to scientific research despite interruptions by military service and war. Nevertheless, he never abandoned his love for science, publishing numerous academic papers during this time and beginning to make his mark in physics. After graduating, he taught at the University of Zurich, finally settling down and escaping the shadows of war to focus on research.

In 1925, Schrödinger was invited to a seminar to explain a doctoral thesis on wave-particle duality. At the seminar, a colleague's question inspired him, and he decided to find a wave equation that could correctly describe the bound electrons of a hydrogen atom.

On January 27, 1926, the academic journal *Annalen der Physik* received a manuscript from Schrödinger. In the paper, he introduced his famous wave equation (the Schrödinger equation below) and wave function, using them to derive the correct energy levels of the hydrogen atom.

$$ i \frac{\partial}{\partial t} \Psi = \hat{H} \Psi $$

Ψ represents the form of the wave. Schrödinger's matter wave equation provides a systematic and quantitative theoretical approach to atomic structure problems, rescuing many physicists. Each microscopic system has a corresponding Schrödinger equation; solving this equation yields the specific form of the wave function. Except for magnetic properties and relativistic effects, Schrödinger's equation can, in principle, explain all atomic phenomena and is the most widely used formula in atomic physics.

It is worth mentioning that the Schrödinger equation is a non-relativistic wave equation and does not account for electron spin. Therefore, for studying microscopic particles involving electron spin and relativistic effects, relativistic quantum mechanics equations should replace them.

This leads us to another fundamental assumption of quantum mechanics: the evolution of the quantum state. The wave function of microscopic particles changes over time according to the Schrödinger equation. A quantum state, used to describe the motion state of particles in quantum mechanics, can be characterized by a set of quantum numbers. One characteristic of quantum states is their superposition and combinability. For example, a particle confined in a box could be on the left or right side of the box.

In layman's terms, wave-particle duality and the wave equation tell us that the state of a quantum can be described by a wave function, and the quantum state provides the approach to solving this wave function. The Schrödinger equation is one of the most fundamental equations in quantum mechanics, with a significance comparable to Newton's equations in classical mechanics.

However, the Schrödinger equation is also an assumption of quantum mechanics, subject to verification through experimentation. The use of the Schrödinger equation is conditional; it requires specifying initial and boundary conditions and ensuring that the wave function satisfies conditions of being single-valued, finite, and continuous while not involving relativistic effects and electron spin. Additionally, while the Schrödinger equation can solve simple systems like the electron in a hydrogen atom, complex systems can only be approximated.

It's important to note that the solution to the Schrödinger equation involves three quantum numbers: the principal, azimuthal, and magnetic quantum numbers. However, to fully describe an electron's state, four quantum numbers are needed: the principal, azimuthal, magnetic, and spin quantum numbers. Though not derivable from the Schrödinger equation, the spin quantum number can be determined experimentally.

While not a perfect equation, the Schrödinger equation still solved the problems faced by physicists at the time and laid the foundation for further research in quantum mechanics. Schrödinger was awarded the Nobel Prize in Physics for his contributions.

2.2.3 Electron Double-Slit Interference: Seeking the Answer to Light

The double-slit interference experiment is considered one of the classics in the history of physics and one of the most peculiar experiments. In fact, before the proposal of wave-particle duality, the double-slit experiment existed to demonstrate the wavelike and particle-like behavior of photons or electrons. Simply put, the experiment can reveal whether light exists in particles or waves.

The experimental setup for double-slit interference is straightforward. The initial version was conducted in 1807 by the English scientist Thomas Young; hence, it's also known as "Young's double-slit experiment." Before this, the physics community firmly believed in Newton's view that light existed in the form of particles. However, Thomas Young maintained that light, similar to sound propagation, could exist as a wave. Young initiated the famous double-slit interference experiment to investigate the true nature of light.

As depicted, initially, Young prepared a candle, a board with two slits, and a wall to conduct his experiment. During the experiment, he lit the candle to create a light source. Then, Young placed the candle in front of the board and observed its projected pattern on the wall. According to the hypothesis, if light were a particle, it would pass directly through the slits and produce two distinct bright spots on the screen. However, if light were a wave, it would interfere like "water waves," resulting in alternating bright and dark stripes on the screen. Young found stripes on the screen, later known as "interference fringes," proving that light existed as a wave.

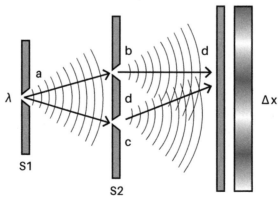

Interference of light

Although Young's initial double-slit experiment in the early 19th century demonstrated that light existed as a wave, this result was not accepted in the physics community at the time. Our modern understanding of light as a wave comes largely from Einstein's photoelectric effect.

Nevertheless, despite initial skepticism, Young's double-slit experiment regained attention with Einstein's proposal of the photoelectric effect and de Broglie's hypothesis of wave-particle duality. Amid escalating controversies, the experiment underwent continuous upgrades, with more physicists revisiting the double-slit experiment to find the "answer to light."

In 1909, Geoffrey Taylor first designed and completed a double-slit interference experiment using a single photon, though it was technically a "feeble light source" rather than a strict single-photon source.

Whether it was a beam of light or a single photon, the material wave nature of light was less intriguing than the material wave nature suggested by de Broglie. Electrons, being particles with mass, were ideal for experiments. In 1961, Claus Jönsson of the University of Tübingen proposed a single-electron double-slit interference experiment. Later, in 1974, Pier Merli and others successfully experimented using a prepared single-electron source. As electrons struck the screen, an image with interference fringes slowly appeared, suggesting that electrons indeed passed through both slits and interfered with themselves. This confirmed that electrons are indeed waves, validating de Broglie's matter wave theory. The discovery of wave-particle duality in microscopic particles spurred the development of electron microscopy, electron diffraction techniques, and neutron diffraction technology, providing more suitable tools to explore and analyze matter's microscopic and crystal structures.

2.2.4 The Puzzling Electron Double-Slit Interference Experiment

The double-slit interference experiment with electrons perfectly demonstrates the wave-particle duality in quantum mechanics. However, the experiment's intrigue extends far beyond this, with even more astonishing discoveries.

Initially, in classical mechanics, when a ball passes through two narrow slits, it can only choose one path, resulting in two distinct marks on the receiving screen—a logical and expected outcome. However, if the slits are very close, the actual image might appear as a large, blurred mark. But when this scenario is scaled down to the quantum level, replacing the ball with microscopic particles like photons or electrons, the results are drastically different. As previously mentioned, regular interference patterns appear on the screen.

The emergence of interference suggests the presence of two entities. However, the particles are emitted one at a time—the next particle is released only after the previous one has reached the screen. Therefore, the interference cannot be a result of interactions between different particles. This leads to the experiment's first peculiar aspect: the particle seems to possess a kind of "clone ability," passing through both slits simultaneously and interfering with itself.

In 1965, American scientist Richard Feynman designed an experiment to determine whether a particle truly exhibits this "clone ability." It involved installing an observation instrument next to the double slits to monitor whether each electron passed through the left or the right slit. Subsequent scientists validated this experiment. They found that if the path of each electron is observed, the electron loses its wave properties, and the interference pattern on the screen disappears, replaced by two spots indicating particle behavior. If observation ceases, the interference condition reappears. In other words, "if you watch it, it behaves like a particle; if you don't, it behaves like a wave." This implies that electrons can somehow sense if they are being observed and exhibit different behaviors accordingly. This is the experiment's second peculiar aspect.

This bizarre phenomenon astonished physicists. The experiment was upgraded to further explore how electrons determine whether they are being observed.

In 1979, at a symposium commemorating Einstein's 100th birthday, the imaginative physicist John Wheeler proposed the concept of a "delayed-choice experiment": What if we could determine which slit a particle passed through after it had already passed through both slits or even after it had hit the screen? Would the interference pattern still exist?

To prevent the particle from "making a decision" in advance, scientists placed the detector behind the slits, allowing the particle to pass through first and then observe which slit it came from. The results mirrored previous findings: if the detector was on, the particle chose one slit; if not, it passed through both.

This was the third and most perplexing aspect of the series of experiments: not only does the particle "know" if it is being observed at the moment, but it also seems to "predict" future observations. It might even be said that upon realizing it is being observed, the particle can alter its past behavior.

Regarded as one of the most bizarre experiments in history, the double-slit interference experiment profoundly altered physicists' understanding of the nature of matter. Eventually, experiments revealed that quantum particles likely exist in a "superposition state" and undergo "quantum collapse." After a photon is emitted from a source, it can exist both as a wave and a particle, simultaneously passing through both the left and right slits. This is the so-called superposition state.

2.3 The Precision Revolution in the Macroscopic World

The discovery of wave-particle duality, along with the electron double-slit interference experiment, though seemingly mystical, has brought significant application insights to quantum theory. One such important application born out of wave-particle duality is quantum measurement.

2.3.1 From Classical to Quantum Measurement

To understand quantum measurement, let us first consider classical measurement based on classical mechanics.

In the world of classical mechanics, that is, in non-quantum physics, "measurement" is defined as obtaining information about certain physical system properties, whether material or immaterial. The information obtained includes velocity, position, energy, temperature, volume, direction, and more.

The classical measurement definition of "measurement" contains two aspects of information: on the one hand, every attribute of a physical system has a certain, even predestined value, determined before the measurement begins. On the other hand, all attributes are measurable, and the information obtained faithfully reflects the measured attribute unaffected by the measurement tools or the observer.

In simple terms, in classical mechanics, the state of an object can be measured, and the interference caused by the measurement act on the measured object is negligible. In other words, whether we measure or not, the physical quantity is there and does not change. For example, to measure the width of a piece of paper, simply comparing it against a ruler yields the result. The paper does not become wider or narrower because of the measurement.

Measurement always involves some degree of error. In such cases, people reduce measurement errors by repeating measurements multiple times or improving technology. However, as demands for measurement precision increase, classical measurement techniques need help to make further improvements. Consequently, scientists have turned their attention to quantum measurement techniques.

The reason lies in classical physics, where we are accustomed to viewing the properties and states of objects as deterministic. This implies that we can accurately determine a physical system's state and properties through measurement. However, this notion of determinism undergoes a fundamental change in the world of quantum mechanics. Quantum mechanics has revolutionized our traditional understanding of matter and natural laws, introducing a new probabilistic description. The core of this concept is uncertainty and wave function collapse.

The randomness of quantum measurement is rooted in the uncertainty principle of quantum mechanics, first proposed by Heisenberg and Schrödinger. This principle indicates that in the quantum world, we cannot precisely determine the position and momentum of a microscopic particle. This means that when we try to measure one attribute of a particle, we inevitably lose precise information about another attribute. For example, if we attempt to reduce the uncertainty in a particle's position, the uncertainty in its momentum will increase, and vice versa. This is why, in the quantum world, we cannot simultaneously know a particle's exact position and momentum.

The wave function is another core concept of quantum measurement. It is a mathematical function used to describe an object's quantum state, including position, momentum, and other physical properties. The wave function is not a trajectory or path of an object but a mathematical tool for describing the probabilities of an object's states. During measurement, the wave function collapses, meaning its properties change, instantly causing the particle's quantum state to collapse to an eigenstate corresponding to the measurement result. This process is random, unlike measurements familiar in classical physics, rendering quantum measurements random. After measurement, the system's quantum state can be well determined and accurately known by observers.

Furthermore, from a quantum perspective, in fields like quantum computing and quantum communication, quantum systems are extremely susceptible to environmental influences, severely constraining the stability and robustness of quantum systems. Quantum measurement cleverly exploits this "weakness" of quantum systems, allowing them to interact with the physical quantity being measured, thereby inducing changes in the quantum state for measurement.

Based on this, by manipulating and measuring quantum states and preparing, controlling, measuring, and reading the quantum states of microscopic particles like atoms, ions, and photons, coupled with data processing and conversion, humanity will leap to a new stage in precision measurement. This will enable ultra-high precision detection of physical quantities like angular velocity, gravitational fields, magnetic fields, and frequencies.

2.3.2 The Three Quantum Measurement Rulers

To enhance measurement precision, the most direct method is to find a "ruler" with a higher resolution. In recent years, utilizing the fundamental properties of quantum mechanics, three types of quantum measurement "rulers" have been developed: measurements based on the energy levels of microscopic particles, measurements based on quantum coherence, and measurements based on quantum entanglement. In fact, these three types represent the evolutionary stages of quantum measurement technology, advancing from discrete energy levels to coherent superposition and then to quantum entanglement, continuously breaking through the limits of classical physics. During this process, the complexity and cost of the systems have increased, as has their size.

Measurement Based on the Energy Levels of Microscopic Particles

Based on Bohr's atomic theory, measurement based on the energy levels of microscopic particles was proposed and was the first to be utilized.

In the early 20th century, Danish physicist Niels Bohr proposed a new atomic model, which successfully explained the spectral line phenomena in the hydrogen atom spectrum. According to this model, electrons orbit the nucleus but can only exist in specific energy states. The emission or absorption of electromagnetic radiation of specific frequencies accompanies transitions between these states. This theory laid the foundation for quantum mechanics and subsequent quantum measurement technology.

Based on Bohr's theory, the transitions between atomic energy levels manifest quantum properties, as these transitions are discrete and relate to specific energy differences. This characteristic provides a unique opportunity for time measurement. Specifically, the electromagnetic waves released by electron transitions in atoms have very stable frequencies, making them extremely accurate time scales.

Following this theory, the second meter in 1967 was redefined at the International Conference on Weights and Measures. Traditionally, a second was defined based on the Earth's rotation period, but this definition needed to be more precise due to the slight variations in the Earth's rotation speed. Therefore, scientists redefined a second based on the period of electron transitions in cesium atoms— one second was redefined as 9,192,631,770 oscillations of the electron transitioning between two energy levels in a cesium atom. This redefinition marked the first major contribution of quantum theory to measurement, providing unprecedented accuracy and stability in time measurement.

Measurement technology based on microscopic particle energy levels provides an accurate benchmark for time measurement and has had a profound impact in other fields. For example, it is key in navigation systems, communication technology, satellite positioning, and Earth science research. Many critical areas of modern society rely on high-precision time measurement, and measurement technology based on microscopic particle energy levels is one of the key tools for achieving this goal.

Measurement Based on Quantum Coherence

Measurement technology based on quantum coherence utilizes the matter-wave properties of quantum particles and interferometry to measure external physical quantities. This technology has been widely applied in manufacturing various instruments and devices, such as gyroscopes, gravimeters, and gravity gradiometers, providing critical support in navigation, geological exploration, aerospace, and other fields and profoundly impacting scientific research and engineering applications.

A core concept of quantum measurement based on coherence is quantum interference, utilizing the wave properties of quantum matter waves. According to quantum mechanics, microscopic particles, like atoms and molecules, possess particle and wave properties. This means their wave functions can propagate and interfere in space like light or sound waves.

In measurement, a device is typically used to split microscopic particles into two interfering wave packets. These wave packets then propagate along different paths and converge at a point, creating interference effects. Adjusting parameters in the measuring device allows interference effects to be controlled, thereby measuring external physical quantities.

Gyroscopes are a classic example of applications utilizing quantum coherence. A gyroscope is an instrument used to measure orientation or angular velocity, exploiting the quantum properties of spin angular momentum. In a gyroscope, two components of spin angular momentum interfere through an interferometric device, and changes in this interference effect can be used to measure the gyroscope's rotation. Quantum coherence-based gyroscopes offer extremely high precision and stability, making them widely used in navigation systems, spacecraft navigation, and geological exploration.

Gravimeters and gravity gradiometers are also typical applications of measurement technology based on quantum coherence. These instruments measure the relative displacement of microscopic particles in the Earth's gravitational field, accurately measuring the Earth's gravity field and gradients, providing key data for geological exploration, earthquake monitoring, and resource exploration. Unlike traditional gravimetric instruments, quantum coherence-based instruments have higher sensitivity and resolution, enabling them to detect subtle geological changes and underground structures.

Measurement Based on Quantum Entanglement

Measurement technology based on quantum entanglement involves measuring the coherent superposition results of N entangled quantum "rulers," achieving a final measurement precision of 1/N of a single quantum "ruler." This represents the highest precision level in the field of quantum measurement. Currently, measurement technology applications based on quantum entanglement have expanded to high-precision quantum clocks, quantum sensors, and quantum computing, bringing enormous potential to scientific research and technology applications and profoundly impacting navigation, communication, precision measurement, and other fields.

The foundation of this measurement technology is quantum entanglement, a special quantum state where multiple quantum particles are highly correlated, regardless of the distance between them. This correlation manifests as measuring one particle's state instantaneously affecting the states of other entangled particles, even without any obvious physical connection. The key principle of measurement technology based on quantum entanglement is to use this entanglement relationship to enhance measurement precision.

Suppose a system comprises N entangled particles, and it is desired to measure a certain physical quantity, such as position or angle. Various errors and uncertainties might influence traditional measurement methods, limiting precision. However, scientists can use their entanglement relationship to improve measurement accuracy by placing these entangled particles in specific quantum states and performing related operations and measurements.

A key advantage of measurement technology based on quantum entanglement is that measurement precision increases with the number of entangled particles N in the system, and the rate of improvement in precision is faster than the increase in N. Specifically, the final measurement precision can reach 1/N of a single quantum particle measurement, a feat unachievable by classical measurement methods. This characteristic gives measurement technology based on quantum entanglement unparalleled potential in high-precision applications.

2.4 Precision Measurement Enters the Quantum Era

The 26th General Conference on Weights and Measures in 2018 officially passed a resolution to implement new definitions of international units from 2019, shifting from physical measurement standards to quantum measurement standards. With this, precision measurement officially entered the quantum era. Currently, quantum measurement is demonstrating broad application prospects, being utilized to detect various physical quantities, including magnetic fields, electric fields, acceleration, angular velocity, gravity, gravity gradients, temperature, time, distance, and more. It is also showing immense potential in numerous fields. Now, research in quantum measurement is mainly focused on five major areas: quantum target recognition, quantum gravity measurement, quantum magnetic field measurement, quantum positioning and navigation, and quantum time-frequency synchronization.

2.4.1 Quantum Target Recognition

Quantum target recognition is an important research direction in the military and defense sectors. Compared to traditional target recognition, quantum measurement technology offers a novel method to detect weak electromagnetic signals or other characteristics emitted by targets. The advantage of this method lies in its exact measurement capability, enabling high-resolution identification of targets, even those employing stealth measures. By measuring the phase, frequency, and intensity of the electromagnetic signals emitted by targets, quantum measurement technology can provide more information to help determine the target's nature and identity.

Moreover, quantum measurement technology's high sensitivity and low noise properties enable the detection of weak signals, even when other interferences mask these signals. Traditional recognition methods may be limited in complex electromagnetic environments or under interference, but quantum measurement technology can operate in high-noise environments, providing reliable results. This is crucial for target recognition on the battlefield, as military operations often involve various electromagnetic interferences and noise.

Additionally, quantum measurement technology can also be applied to satellite recognition. Satellites play a significant role in modern military communications, navigation, and intelligence gathering. Quantum measurement technology can be used to determine the type, orbit, and mission of satellites by measuring the characteristics of signals emitted by satellites. This is important for strategic planning and decision-making in national defense security and intelligence warfare.

2.4.2 Quantum Gravity Measurement

Quantum gravity measurement is a significant application in Earth science and resource exploration. It leverages quantum measurement technology's high precision and sensitivity to measure subtle variations in gravitational fields, thus providing tools and methods for geological exploration, resource prospecting, and environmental monitoring.

Specifically, in Earth science research and resource exploration, measuring and analyzing gravitational fields are crucial for understanding underground geological structures and detecting mineral deposits, water resources, oil and gas reservoirs, and underground formations. Traditional methods of gravity measurement have played a significant role in these areas, but they face certain limitations when dealing with weak signals, complex geological conditions, or deep structures.

The introduction of quantum measurement technology offers new solutions to these challenges. First, the high precision of quantum measurement technology enables the detection of minute changes in gravitational fields, even when these changes are extremely subtle. This holds immense potential for discovering underground minerals, water resources, and pipelines. Quantum measurement technology allows for high-resolution measurements of subsurface material distribution and density changes, thereby enhancing the efficiency and accuracy of resource exploration.

Second, the high sensitivity of quantum measurement technology enables the detection of minor geological changes, including underground faults, rock formations, and water flows. This is of significant importance for research in geological science and environmental monitoring. By monitoring subtle changes in underground gravitational fields, scientists can better understand Earth processes such as crustal movement, seismic activity, and the hydrological cycle, aiding in the early warning of geological disasters and environmental changes.

Additionally, quantum measurement technology is non-invasive and highly efficient, making it an ideal tool for subsurface exploration. Traditional methods of underground exploration may require drilling or seismic surveys, which are time-consuming, labor-intensive, and expensive. In contrast, quantum measurement technology allows for non-invasive measurements at the surface without damaging the underground environment, thus reducing exploration costs and environmental impact.

2.4.3 Quantum Magnetic Field Measurement

As the name suggests, quantum magnetic field measurement, based on quantum theory, is already being applied in fields such as Earth science, mineral exploration, and medical imaging.

The Earth's magnetic field is a vital indicator of its internal structure and geodynamics. By measuring the Earth's magnetic field, scientists can study the evolution of the Earth's magnetic field, the properties of its core and mantle, and crustal structures. Traditional geomagnetic measurement methods typically require placing numerous magnetometers at the surface and conducting fixed-point measurements. Quantum magnetic field measurement technology, however, enables high-precision, real-time magnetic field measurements. This not only improves measurement efficiency but also expands the measurement range, aiding in a better understanding of the Earth's complex magnetic field distribution.

In the field of mineral exploration, there is a huge demand for magnetic field measurements. When searching for mineral deposits and mineral resources, the magnetic characteristics of the subsurface are often associated with the presence of minerals. Traditional magnetic measurement methods typically use magnetometers, but their resolution and accuracy are limited. Quantum magnetic field measurement technology allows for high-resolution measurements of subtle magnetic features, helping to locate and explore mineral deposits, thereby enhancing the efficiency and success rate of resource exploration more accurately.

The field of medical imaging has also benefited from the development of quantum magnetic field measurement technology. Magnetic Resonance Imaging (MRI) is a common medical diagnostic method that uses magnetic fields and radio waves to create images of the human body's interior. Quantum magnetic field measurement technology can improve the sensitivity and resolution of MRI, enabling more precise detection of internal body structures and abnormalities and providing more reliable data for medical diagnosis.

2.4.4 Quantum Positioning and Navigation

The concept of navigation has existed since ancient times, from astral navigation in the Stone Age to geomagnetic navigation during the age of sail, guiding the way for early travelers. With the advancement of space technology, electronic information technology, computer science, and optical communication, these ancient navigation methods have evolved over the past few decades into various navigation systems represented by radio navigation and inertial navigation, making Positioning,

Navigation, and Timing (PNT) functionalities completer and more mature. Moreover, with the development of modern warfare based on location, time, and other information, as well as autonomous driving technologies, navigation demands have become more stringent. For high-requirement navigation systems, traditional positioning techniques' safety, vulnerability, and ultimate precision are increasingly scrutinized. Although navigation technology based on satellite communication has improved precision, it still falls short of meeting the high accuracy required for autonomous driving.

Consequently, scientists have begun exploring navigation methods based on quantum communication, also known as Quantum Positioning System (QPS). The concept of QPS was first introduced in 2001 by Dr. Giovannetti Vittorio, Dr. Maccone Lorenzo, and Professor Lloyd Seth, a mechanical engineering professor specializing in quantum computing and quantum communication at MIT, in their paper "Quantum-Enhanced Positioning and Clock Synchronization." Currently, the UK's Defense Science and Technology Laboratory (DSTL) is researching a type of accelerometer based on ultra-cold atoms capable of unprecedented precision in tracking human movement. Traditional GPS fails underwater, so when submarines submerge, they lose GPS signals and must navigate using accelerometers, recording each turn and twist. However, accelerometers are imprecise. Without GPS, a submarine could deviate about 1 km from its course in a day's travel, but QPS could reduce this deviation to about 1 m.

The technical principle of DSTL's research involves using lasers to capture a cloud of atoms in a vacuum and cool it to just above absolute zero. At such low temperatures, atoms enter a quantum state easily disrupted by external forces. The magnitude of the external force can be calculated by tracking any changes caused by disturbances with another laser beam. Since submarines sway slightly due to the action of seawater, causing minor deviations, the DSTL team hopes to use this system in underwater environments.

QPS, based on quantum mechanics and information theory, is a new generation of navigation and positioning technology developed in recent years. In this system, information generation, measurement, and transmission all involve quantum processes. Due to phenomena like quantum entanglement and quantum collapse, it offers unique advantages regarding the secrecy, safety, and measurement precision of information transmission. It can also achieve precise communication in areas unreachable by traditional GPS or satellite communication.

The main application areas of quantum positioning and navigation are in modern warfare for precise guidance and strikes and in transportation, particularly in autonomous driving technology. In fields like missile strikes, aerospace, maritime, and vehicle navigation, high-precision positioning and navigation systems are crucial for ensuring safety and improving efficiency. Based on this, quantum measurement technology can use precise time and distance measurements to achieve highly accurate location information, providing more reliable data for navigation systems.

For instance, in 2018, the UK developed a QPS based on quantum accelerometers. In submarine travel, using traditional inertial navigation systems, the deviation could reach about 1 km in a day, whereas with QPS, the deviation is only about 1 m per day.

2.4.5 Quantum Time-Frequency Synchronization

In modern warfare, communication, financial transactions, scientific research, high-precision clocks, and frequency synchronization are crucial. Quantum measurement technology can utilize the entanglement relationships between quantum states to achieve highly precise time and frequency measurements, providing key support for the security of communication networks and the stability of data transmission.

For example, in the field of communication, traditional communication systems rely on precise clock synchronization to coordinate the sending and receiving of data. However, during transmission, clock synchronization may experience errors due to signal propagation delays and noise interference, leading to instability and loss of data transmission. Quantum measurement technology can achieve highly precise clock synchronization by measuring the temporal correlations between quantum states, enhancing the data transmission rate and security of communication systems. Moreover, quantum communication technologies such as Quantum Key Distribution (QKD) also rely on accurate time synchronization to ensure encryption and security of communication.

Additionally, financial transactions require precise time stamps and frequency control to ensure the accuracy and traceability of orders. In high-frequency trading and global financial markets, even millisecond or microsecond differences in timing can lead to significant transaction losses. Quantum measurement technology can provide highly stable clock and frequency synchronization, ensuring the accuracy and fairness of financial transactions. Furthermore, financial security applications such as quantum secure guards and quantum random number generation also depend on quantum time-frequency synchronization to protect the security of financial information.

Especially in modern warfare, precision in strikes is about location accuracy and timing accuracy, where temporal precision often takes precedence. Therefore, high-precision communication technology based on quantum technology builds a more secure remote-control capability and, more importantly, can achieve time control that is more precise, or closer to absolute precision, than traditional concepts of time.

It is evident that the application fields of quantum measurement technology are very broad, covering basic scientific research, military defense, aerospace, energy exploration, transportation, disaster early warning, and many other areas. In the future, as quantum measurement technology continues to innovate and be applied, it will play an increasingly important role in even more fields.

2.5 Magnetometers Moving toward "Quantization"

Magnetism is a fundamental physical property in nature, present in everything from microscopic particles to celestial bodies. From ancient compasses to modern Gauss meters and superconducting quantum interference devices (SQUIDs), magnetic measurement technology has continually evolved with scientific advancements. Quantum magnetometers, based on quantum theory, are now one of the main representatives in the quantum precision measurement industry.

2.5.1 Different Technological Approaches to Quantum Magnetometers

Quantum magnetometers have developed several technological approaches, the most significant being nuclear precession magnetometers, SQUIDs, atomic magnetometers, and Diamond Nitrogen-Vacancy (NV) Center magnetometers.

Nuclear precession magnetometers are based on the principle of Nuclear Magnetic Resonance (NMR). They use the precession movement of atomic nuclei in external magnetic fields to measure the strength and direction of magnetic fields. These magnetometers are widely used in medical imaging (MRI), NMR spectroscopy, and geophysical research.

SQUID magnetometers are based on superconducting materials and utilize quantum interference effects in superconducting loops to detect minute changes in magnetic fields. Depending on the superconducting material used, SQUIDs can be low-temperature or high-temperature; they are further classified into direct current (DC) and radio frequency (RF) SQUIDs based on the number of the Josephson junction in the loop. SQUID magnetometers have extremely high sensitivity and are used to measure weak magnetic fields such as brain activity, the Earth's magnetic field, and material magnetism.

Atomic magnetometers utilize the quantum properties of atoms and optical methods to measure magnetic fields, including optical pumping and Coherent Population Trapping measurements.

Diamond NV center magnetometers, a type of solid-state quantum sensor, have attracted attention due to their high spatial resolution capabilities. The principle involves the coherent manipulation of single electron spin qubits, where NV centers in diamond crystals act as quantum bits whose electron spins couple with external magnetic fields. Notably, they do not require cooling to low temperatures and ensure biocompatibility with high sensitivity, making them widely applicable in biomolecular research and fundamental physics. The biological signal imaging with this material theoretically approaches the optical diffraction limit, offering excellent spatial resolution.

Currently, magnetic measurement technology based on single NV centers has achieved nanoscale resolution and sensitivity capable of detecting single nuclear spins. In 2015, Professor Du Jiangfeng's team from the University of Science and Technology of China used NV centers as quantum probes to obtain the world's first magnetic resonance spectrum of a single protein molecule under room-temperature atmospheric conditions. This research advanced magnetic resonance technology from billions of molecules to a single molecule and established a "room temperature atmosphere" as a viable experimental environment for widespread future applications in life sciences, enabling high-resolution nanoscale MRI and diagnostics.

Unlike single NV center magnetic measurement technology, ensemble NV center magnetic measurement usually targets macroscopic magnetic fields. In applications, ensemble NV center magnetometers have detected magnetic signals from worm neurons, eddy current imaging, and ancient geomagnetic studies in mineralogy.

It's worth noting that each type of quantum magnetometer has advantages and disadvantages in various characteristics, and each excels in different application scenarios. Based on quantum spin technology, Diamond NV center magnetometers and atomic magnetometers are among the most promising quantum sensors for commercialization in recent years, with diverse industry and application scenarios.

2.5.2 Advancing toward the Medical Field

In life science research, physical quantities like light, electricity, heat, and magnetism are critical for measurement, with optical imaging being the most widely used. However, optical imaging often needs to be improved due to strong background signals in biological samples, unstable fluorescence signals, and difficulty in absolute quantification, affecting detection accuracy.

MRI, with its penetrating, low-background, non-invasive, and stable characteristics, promises to address these shortcomings of optical imaging. However, it is limited by low sensitivity and spatial resolution, making it challenging to apply at tissue-level imaging with micron-to-nanometer resolution. In this context, the recently developed diamond NV center magnetometers offer a new technical solution.

NV center-based magnetic imaging technology can detect weak magnetic signals with nanoscale spatial resolution and non-invasiveness. It provides a flexible and compatible magnetic field measurement platform for the life sciences. It enables tissue-level research and clinical diagnostics in immunology and inflammation, neurodegenerative diseases, cardiovascular diseases, biomagnetic sensing, and magnetic resonance contrast agents. It is particularly advantageous for biological tissues with optical backgrounds, poor light transmission, and requiring quantitative analysis.

In magnetic imaging, NV center-based magnetic imaging technology primarily includes scanning magnetic imaging and wide-field magnetic imaging. Scanning magnetic imaging combines with AFM technology, using single-color diamond sensors for point-scanning imaging with high spatial resolution and sensitivity. However, its imaging speed and range limit its application in some areas. Wide-field magnetic imaging uses ensemble diamond sensors. Though high-density NV centers reduce spatial resolution compared to single NV centers, they show great potential in wide-field, real-time imaging.

For example, in the application of magnetotactic bacteria imaging. Magnetotactic bacteria are a type of bacteria that move directionally under external magnetic fields and form nanoscale magnetic particles—magnetosomes—inside their bodies. Placing bacteria on a diamond surface and using optical methods to detect the quantum spin state of NV centers makes it possible to rapidly reconstruct images of the magnetic field vector components produced by magnetosomes in bacteria. Wide-field magnetic imaging microscopes can perform optical and magnetic imaging of multiple cells simultaneously with sub-micrometer resolution in a large field of view. This work provides a new method for imaging biological magnetic structures within living cells at high spatial resolution and makes mapping extensive magnetic signals within cells and cell networks possible.

Another example is in immune magnetic labeling cell imaging. Cancer, one of the leading causes of human death, requires research into its molecular mechanisms and early, precise clinical diagnosis for effective treatment. The research team from the University of Science and Technology of China developed a tissue-level immune magnetic labeling method, specifically marking target proteins such as PD-L1 in tumor tissues with superparamagnetic particles through antigen-antibody recognition. Then, placing tissue samples close to the diamond surface, they used the layer of NV centers near the surface as a two-dimensional quantum magnetic sensor to perform magnetic field imaging on an NV wide-field microscope with 400 nm resolution, achieving micrometer spatial resolution in a millimeter field of view. Finally, they reconstructed the magnetic moment distribution corresponding to the magnetic field through a deep learning model, laying the foundation for quantitative analysis.

Previously, the Harvard-Smithsonian Center for Astrophysics used immune magnetic labeling technology and NV wide-field magnetic imaging technology to compare the magnetic imaging of cancer cells and healthy cells, proving the practicality of the imaging technology and providing an important tool for biomedical cell detection.

2.6   Making Time Precise to One Quintillionth

Understanding and measuring time is an ancient discipline. The ancient concept of "four corners and up and down as the universe, the past and the present as the time" reflects a primitive notion of space and time. An astronomical calendar based on astronomical time has always been a significant hallmark of civilization. In the agricultural era, the precision of the calendar significantly impacted social life. Sociologist Lewis Mumford stated, "The key machine of the modern industrial age is the clock, not the steam engine."

If the clock was the key machine of the industrial age, it remains so in the information age. Without modern clocks, computers, the defining machines of the information era, could not exist. Clocks synchronize human behavior and determine the speed of the billions of operations a computer performs each second. In the information age, the demand for clock precision has increased, and quantum measurement meets the new requirements for more precise time measurement.

2.6.1 Time Measurement under Quantum Theory

A clock's accuracy comes from its time base. For a pendulum clock, the time base is the pendulum.

Over 600 years ago, Galileo inadvertently discovered that the swinging time of a chandelier in a church was always similar. Galileo's insights made Huygens the first to create a high-quality pendulum clock. In 1657, Huygens designed a clock that represented a significant leap in timekeeping technology. Before that, the best clocks deviated about 15 minutes per day; Huygens's clock had a daily error of only 10 seconds.

Although ideally, the only factors determining a pendulum's swing are its length and Earth's gravitational acceleration, even slight variations, given Earth's near-perfect sphericity and almost constant acceleration due to gravity, can accumulate and affect a pendulum clock's precision. Thus, in the mid-19th century, increasingly precise mechanical clocks were developed based on pendulum clocks, achieving timing accuracy that met daily needs.

From the 1930s, with the invention of the crystal oscillator, small, low-energy quartz crystal clocks replaced mechanical clocks, widely used in electronic timers and other timing areas until now, becoming the main timekeeping devices in daily life.

Different from pendulum clocks, the time base of a quartz clock is a small quartz crystal. When voltage is applied to a quartz crystal, it vibrates at a high frequency. The vibration frequency depends on several factors, including the crystal's type and shape, but typically, the quartz crystal in a digital watch vibrates at a frequency of 32,768 hertz. Digital circuits count these vibrations to record every passing second. However, more is needed for the rapidly evolving information age.

Modern electronic computers perform calculations in fractions of a second, ranging from tens of millions to hundreds of millions and even billions of a second. Modern technology requires a more precise international standard time: a one-second error could cause a navigator using a sextant to be off course by 1/4 mile; a 1‰ second difference could send a spacecraft 10 m off course; every second, a computer can perform 800,000 calculations.

To meet the demand for precise time in the information age, from the 1940s, clockmaking turned toward atomic clocks based on quantum theory. Atomic clocks have become the most accurate clocks in the world—electrons inside atoms emit electromagnetic waves when they transition, and their transition frequency is extremely stable. These electromagnetic waves are used to control electronic oscillators, and thus the movement of the clock is the principle behind atomic clocks.

Specifically, atoms, such as cesium, have a resonance frequency, meaning electromagnetic radiation at this frequency will cause them to "vibrate"—the "orbiting" electrons transition to a higher energy level. Cesium-133 isotopes resonate when stimulated by microwave radiation at a precise frequency of 9,192,631,770 hertz. This radiation frequency is the time base of atomic clocks, with cesium atoms serving as calibrators to ensure the frequency's accuracy. In this context, the 13th General Conference on Weights and Measures in 1967 redefined the "second" as "the duration of 9,192,631,770 periods of radiation corresponding to the transition between two hyperfine energy levels of the cesium atom."

The accuracy of atomic clocks is almost unimaginable for Huygens. His pendulum clocks might have a daily error of 10 seconds, whereas an atomic clock that started timing 4.5 billion years ago when Earth was formed would have an error of less than 10 seconds today.

The world's first atomic clock—the ammonia clock—was made by the National Bureau of Standards in the United States in 1949, marking a new era in timekeeping and time-setting. In the following decades, atomic clock technology significantly developed, with the creation of rubidium, cesium, and hydrogen clocks, among others. By 1992, atomic clocks were widely used worldwide.

2.6.2 From Atomic Clocks to Cold Atom Clocks

Alongside the development of atomic clocks, the advancement of laser cooling atomic technology is further enhancing the precision of time measurement with the creation of cold atom clocks. Cold atom clocks increase precision by reducing the temperature of atoms, thereby minimizing external disturbances on atomic transition frequencies.

The most accurate atomic clocks cool atoms to temperatures near zero, slowing their thermal motion with lasers and detecting them in a microwave-filled cavity. Measuring these nearly stationary atoms results in greater accuracy—the most precise ground-based cold atom fountain clocks now have an error rate of 1 second in 300 million years, and even more precise cold-atom optical clocks are rapidly developing.

The next step for cold atom clocks is to move into space. Unlike terrestrial cold atom clocks, space-based ones primarily utilize the microgravity environment of space. In microgravity, atomic clusters can move in ultra-slow uniform linear motion. Atoms in a pure quantum ground state pass through a ring-shaped microwave cavity, interacting twice with a separated microwave field to produce a quantum superposition state. The ratio of atoms in two quantum states is measured by a dual energy-level detector, obtaining the atomic transition probability. Changing the microwave frequency yields the Ramsay fringes of the atomic clock, which can be fed back to the local oscillator to obtain a high-precision time-frequency standard signal. Chinese scientists are actively developing the next generation of higher-precision space-based microwave atomic clocks, achieving the first space cold atom clock using laser cooling technology internationally in 2018.

Simultaneously, breakthroughs in quantum precision measurement methods have led scientists to develop new types of atomic clocks like strontium and ytterbium. Operating at higher frequencies in the optical spectrum, they are called "optical atomic clocks" or "optical clocks." Optical clocks now have a measurement precision of one quintillionth (10^{-19}), with less than a second's error over the entire age of the universe.

In the past 20 years, optical clock technology has rapidly advanced. For instance, the strontium atomic optical clock developed by the National Institute of Standards and Technology (NIST) in the USA has reached an uncertainty level of 10^{-18} and a stability of 10^{-19}, advancing at least two orders of magnitude over microwave atomic clocks. Chinese scientists have developed a calcium ion optical clock reaching uncertainties and stabilities in the 10^{-18} range. China has also planned the development of space optical clocks, aiming to improve time-frequency measurement precision in space by two orders of magnitude.

2.6.3 What Does the Innovation in Time Precision Bring?

Time, as one of the seven fundamental physical quantities, is currently the most precisely measured. The continuous exploration in theory and technology to improve time measurement precision aims at what?

The most direct change is a new understanding of the world. Over a century ago, the famous physicist Lord Kelvin suggested that "the future of physics lies in the sixth decimal place," highlighting the significance of precision metrology. 2005 Nobel Laureate in Physics John Hall even said, "Metrology is the mother of science." Accurate measurement and transmission of time will allow for experimental verification of relativity principles, various gravitational theories, dark matter models, and other fundamental physics. Even slight differences in measurement results might lead to a shift in our understanding of space and time.

Moreover, innovations in time precision will impact technological development. For example, the accuracy of satellite navigation is closely related to time-keeping precision. Our lives now heavily depend on navigation and positioning, and for more accurate positioning, such as to the meter or less, better timekeeping precision is needed.

Just as the most advanced clocks of the 18th and 19th centuries revolutionized maritime navigation, atomic and optical clocks of the information age have revolutionized navigation. Global Positioning Navigation Systems (like the US GPS) established on this basis now cover 98% of the Earth's surface.

Whether in our smartphones or on missile heads, GPS can determine location by measuring the distance from at least four satellites to a receiver on Earth. Signals sent from satellites 20,000 km away at the speed of light take about 66 milliseconds to reach us. A 10 m movement would require an additional 33 nanoseconds (0.000000033 seconds).

GPS receivers must capture such minuscule differences between transmission and arrival times. To achieve this, GPS not only needs to launch several satellites into space but also place an atomic clock on each one. By measuring the time differences in signals from different satellites, GPS receivers can triangulate their latitude, longitude, and altitude. Today's atomic clocks and GPS satellites not only tell us where we are but also precisely when we are there.

Apart from enhancing autonomous operation and navigation precision in navigation positioning systems, atomic clocks have opened a new phase in scientific exploration.

In fundamental physics research, high-precision time measurement is crucial for advancing measurements of fundamental physical constants, verification of general relativity, and precision metrology, such as gravitational redshift measurements, gravitational wave detection, anisotropy of the speed of light, gravitational gradient measurements, and dark matter. After all, "time" has become the most accurately measured fundamental physical quantity in modern science and technology. The precision of other fundamental physical quantities like length, magnetic fields, electric fields, and temperature can be improved through various physical conversions, forming the basis of modern physical metrology.

Humanity has embarked on an expedition to continually enhance the accuracy of time measurement. From quartz to atomic clocks, this precise revolution may lead humanity into a new world where our understanding of time will be redefined.

2.7   Quantum Measurement: A Burgeoning Field

Research in quantum precision measurement is underway in several countries and regions worldwide, focusing on enhancing measurement performance, challenging precision records, and breaking classical measurement limits. Efforts are being made to advance prototype system engineering, furthering miniaturization, chip integration, and mobility to enhance practicality and achieve breakthroughs.

2.7.1 The Global Race in Quantum Measurement

Quantum measurement has garnered widespread attention globally, especially for its potential applications in fundamental research, aerospace, biomedicine, inertial guidance, and energy exploration. Governments worldwide are accelerating their efforts in quantum measurement, intensifying research and development.

The United States, as early as 2016, proposed ten "Big Ideas" as a long-term research plan, including the "Quantum Leap: Leading the Next Quantum Revolution" initiative aimed at achieving more efficient computing, communication, sensing, and simulation. The Defense Advanced Research Projects Agency (DARPA) established Small Business Innovation Research and Small Business Technology Transfer programs to support research in over a dozen technology areas, including quantum sensing and metrology. In December 2020, the US Air Force allocated $35 million for quantum research, supporting eight quantum measurement companies like AOSense. DARPA's Micro-PNT Program also supports research in chip-scale atomic clocks, integrated micro-primary atomic clocks (cold atom clocks), and quantum gyroscopes, developing miniaturized, chip-scale positioning, navigation, and timing systems, focusing on passive navigation technology to maintain high-precision capabilities even when GPS is denied. The US Department of Defense's "Atomic Clocks with Enhanced Stability" (ACES) Project aims to develop the next generation of chip-scale atomic clocks with a thousandfold performance improvement.

The European Quantum Technologies Flagship, established in 2018, brings together research institutions, industry, and public funders to promote the development of the European quantum industry and turn quantum research into commercial applications and disruptive technologies. In February 2020, the EU's Quantum Flagship progress report highlighted quantum sensing and metrology technologies focusing on pressure, temperature, gravity, magnetic field measurements, clock synchronization, positioning, navigation, and ultra-high-resolution imaging, impacting medical, physical, chemical, biological, geophysical, climate, and environmental sciences. The European Quantum Flagship launched 20 research projects, with four directly related to quantum measurement: macQsimal (developing micro atomic vapor cell quantum devices for sensing and metrology), MetaboliQs (using room-temperature diamond quantum dynamics for safe multimodal cardiac imaging), iqClock (integrated quantum clock), and ASTERIQS (diamond quantum sensing technology).

The UK Quantum Technologies Strategic Advisory Board initiated the National Quantum Technologies Program with a £120 million investment to establish four quantum technology hubs. The UK National Quantum Technology Hub focuses on quantum sensors and measurement technology for defense, geophysics, medical diagnostics, construction, naval navigation, data storage hosts, health monitoring, gaming interfaces, GPS replacement, local network timing, and gravity imaging. The Quantum Imaging Hub focuses on new ultra-high sensitivity cameras, including single-photon visible and infrared cameras, single-pixel cameras, extreme temporal resolution imaging, 3D contouring, hyperspectral, ultra-low flux covert illumination, beyond visual range imaging, and local gravitational field imaging. Plans include investing £94 million over five years to refresh the quantum technology hubs and maintain the UK's leadership established through the National Quantum Technologies Program.

Germany's "Quantum Technologies—from Basics to Market" program allocated €650 million for quantum technology R&D and commercialization from 2018 to 2022. The focus includes measurement technology for high-performance, secure data networks, among many technology areas, laying a solid academic and economic foundation for quantum technology development.

Japan's Ministry of Education announced the Quantum Leap Flagship Program (Q-LEAP), which funds scientific research in quantum optics and supports three technology areas, including quantum measurement and sensors, with one fundamental research project and two flagship projects in each area. Basic research projects receive ¥20–¥30 million annually, while flagship projects receive ¥300–¥400 million. Two flagship projects in quantum measurement and sensors focus on solid-state quantum sensors and quantum optical sensors.

In China, the Political Bureau of the Central Committee of CPC held its 24th collective study session on the prospects of quantum science research and applications on October 16, 2020. Academician Xue Qikun explained the topic, offering opinions and suggestions. President Xi Jinping delivered an important speech outlining strategic plans and systematic arrangements for China's quantum science development in the current and future periods. The "14th Five-Year" plan adopted at the fifth plenary session of the 19th CPC Central Committee also mentioned implementing a batch of forward-looking, strategic national major science and technology projects in frontier areas such as quantum information. Since December 2020, various provinces and cities have successfully issued "14th Five-Year" plans and suggestions, proposing accelerating breakthroughs in core key technologies and advancing quantum science. Anhui Province specifically mentioned accelerating the formation of a quantum information industry innovation chain, creating a globally influential "Quantum Center," and actively laying out integrated space and ground quantum precision measurement experimental facilities.

However, in many areas of quantum measurement, China still needs to catch up to international advanced levels. Several Western companies have launched commercial products based on cold atoms, including gravimeters, frequency standards (clocks), accelerometers, and gyroscopes, and are actively developing emerging fields like quantum computing. Representative quantum sensing and measurement companies include AOSense, a US-based innovative atomic optical sensor manufacturer focusing on high-precision navigation, time and frequency standards, and gravity measurement research, with products like commercial compact quantum gravimeters and cold atom frequency standards, collaborating with NASA and other institutions.

Quspin, also in the US, announced the development of miniaturized SERF atomic magnetometers in 2013 and launched its second-generation product in 2019, with a probe size of 5cm^3, further advancing toward magnetoencephalography array systems. Geometrics, dedicated to seismometers and atomic magnetometers, has released several land-based and airborne geomagnetic measurement products. France's Muquans develops a wide product range for quantum inertial sensing, high-performance time and frequency applications, and advanced laser solutions, with products like absolute quantum gravimeters and cold atom frequency standards, starting quantum computing processor research in 2020.

MSquaredLasers in the UK develops inertial sensors and quantum timing devices for gravity, acceleration, and rotation, including quantum accelerometers, quantum gravimeters, and optical lattice clocks, also venturing into quantum computing with neutral atoms and ions.

In contrast, China's quantum measurement applications and industrialization are still in the initial stages, lagging behind Western countries. At the forefront of optical clock research, China's prototype accuracy indicators are two orders of magnitude behind international levels. Chinese NMR gyro prototypes have gaps in size and accuracy. There are also disparities in quantum target recognition research and systematic integration, significant gaps in microwave band quantum detection technology research, and quantum gravimeters are approaching performance indicators. However, they are still in the initial stages of engineering and miniaturization product development.

China's more mature quantum measurement products are mainly concentrated in the quantum time-frequency synchronization field. Chengdu Spaceon Elect Co.

specializes in time-frequency and Beidou satellite application products, with atomic clocks as its main product. Additionally, research institutions under CETC, CASC, CASIC, and CSIC are gradually conducting quantum measurement research in their respective areas of expertise.

2.7.2 Quantum Measurement Moving toward Commercialization

Quantum measurement has now entered a phase of commercialization.

From an industry development perspective, global quantum measurement market revenues are growing annually. A BCC Research report noted that the global quantum measurement market has a Compound Annual Growth Rate (CAGR) of about 10% in recent years, with expectations to grow to about $300 million in the 2020–2025 period.

In this market, atomic clocks, gravimeters, and magnetometers are more developed and technologically mature, occupying the majority of the quantum measurement market share. According to ICV data, in 2022, the atomic clock market share is approximately $440 million, the highest at 46.3%, with a CAGR of about 4.9% (2022–2029); followed by quantum magnetic measurement, with a market share of about $250 million, CAGR around 6.2% (2022–2029); then quantum scientific and industrial instruments, with a market share of about $200 million, CAGR around 4.4% (2022–2029); and finally, quantum gravimetry, with a market share of about $60 million, CAGR around 5.4% (2022–2029).

Geographically, the main global suppliers are concentrated in North America (mainly the United States), accounting for about 47%; followed by Europe (mainly Western European countries and Russia), accounting for about 28%; and then Asia-Pacific (Japan, South Korea, China, Australia, and Singapore), accounting for about 21%. The US and Western European countries are major technology exporters and purchasers. International companies involved in quantum measurement technology include AOSense, μQuans, Twinleaf, Oscilloquartz, Northrop Grumman, etc., with products like quantum accelerometers, clock sources, radar imaging, magnetometers, gyroscopes, and gravimeters widely used in aerospace, military, telecommunications, energy exploration, medical detection, and many other fields.

In the Asia-Pacific region, particularly China, the demand for quantum measurement products is expected to dominate in the future. As remote healthcare, industrial Internet, Internet of Things (IoT), IoV, autonomous robots, microsatellites, and other technologies and applications mature in China, the demand for ultra-precise, miniaturized, low-cost sensors, biological detectors, positioning and navigation systems, and other devices is expected to grow significantly, presenting substantial market potential.

2.7.3 Standardization Issues Yet to Be Resolved

As quantum measurement enters the industrialization phase, standardization needs to be addressed.

Current research on standardization in quantum measurement mainly focuses on early-stage pre-research, such as terminology definitions, application models, and technology evolution. The standard system has not been established, and enterprise participation is low. Given the multitude of technical directions and application areas in quantum measurement, where terminology, index systems, and testing methods significantly differ, standardization research in quantum measurement is necessary to aid application development, testing, validation, and industry promotion.

For technologies that have entered prototyping or early practicalization, conducting standardization research in overall technical requirements, evaluation systems, testing methods, and component interfaces is essential.

However, today, standardization in the field of quantum measurement has only begun in scattered areas, and comprehensive standardization is yet to be fully implemented. For example, ITU-T's Focus Group on Quantum Information Technology for Networks (FG-QIT4N) and IETF's Quantum Internet Research Group are researching quantum time-frequency synchronization applications in networks. In China, TC578 (National Technical Committee for Quantum Computing and Measurement Standardization) has initiated research projects on quantum inertial measurement testing methods. The China Communications Standards Association (CCSA) ST7 Quantum Communications and Information Technology Task Group under the Quantum Information Processing Working Group (WG2) has launched research projects on applying quantum time synchronization technology in communication networks.

In summary, the quantum measurement industry is in its early stages of development. Before large-scale applications emerge, quantum measurement requires collaborative efforts across multiple sectors to advance technology development and industry promotion and turn research findings into commercial products.

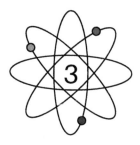

THE ESSENCE OF QUANTUM

3.1 Breaking the "Ugly Duckling Theorem"

In 1923, Louis de Broglie proposed in his doctoral thesis that the particle behavior of light and the wave behavior of particles should correspondingly exist, thus giving birth to the hypothesis of wave-particle duality. He linked a particle's wavelength to its momentum: the greater the momentum, the shorter the wavelength. At the time, it was a captivating idea, even though no one knew what the wave nature of particles meant or how it related to atomic structure. Nonetheless, de Broglie's hypothesis became an important prelude to quantum theory entering a new stage, changing many things.

On the foundation of de Broglie's wave-particle duality, in the summer of 1924, Satyendra N. Bose proposed a novel method to explain the law of blackbody radiation. Bose envisioned light as a gas composed of massless particles (now called photons), which did not follow the classical Boltzmann statistical law but a new statistical theory based on the indistinguishability of particles (their identical nature). This indistinguishability of particles further propagated quantum theory and became a crucial component of the new quantum theory.

3.1.1 An Error That Wasn't Wrong

The "Ugly Duckling Theorem" suggests that the difference between two swans is the same as between an ugly duckling and a swan, implying that no two things in the world are completely identical. However, in the microscopic world, two electrons are entirely identical. And it was Bose who first proposed this concept.

Bose, less renowned compared to Planck, Einstein, Schrödinger, or de Broglie, was born in Kolkata, India. His father was a railway engineer, and Bose was the eldest of seven children. He received appreciation and guidance from several excellent teachers during his university years but only earned a master's degree in mathematics, not pursuing a doctorate. He immediately became a lecturer in physics in Kolkata, later moving to the University of Dhaka, where he self-studied physics.

As a third-world physicist, Bose faced many limitations. Still, his research on Bose-Einstein statistics secured him a significant place in the development of quantum theory, and it was the only major achievement of his life.

Interestingly, Bose discovered the Bose-Einstein statistics due to an "error." Around 1922, while teaching about the photoelectric effect and the ultraviolet catastrophe in blackbody radiation, he intended to show his students the discrepancies between theoretical predictions and experimental results. At that time, the new quantum theory had not yet emerged, and the old quantum theory, used for over twenty years, was merely quantum adjustments within the framework of classical physics. For the statistical behavior of particles, classical Boltzmann statistics were still applied.

Back then, the concept of "distinguishable or indistinguishable" particles did not exist. Each classical particle, with its precise trackable orbit, meant that all classical particles were distinguishable. Like others, Bose intended to clarify the inconsistency between blackbody radiation theory and experiments to his students. He used classical statistics to derive theoretical formulas but made an error akin to "the probability of getting two heads when tossing two coins is one-third." Surprisingly, this error led to conclusions consistent with experiments—a statistical law for indistinguishable, identical particles.

Let's first look at the mistake Bose made in probability. Normally, if we toss two coins since each coin has two distinct sides, there are four possible outcomes: heads-heads, heads-tails, tails-heads, and tails-tails. If we assume each outcome is equally likely, then the probability of each is one-fourth.

However, if these two coins become some "indistinguishable" particles—meaning they are completely identical and thus indistinguishable—"heads-tails" and "tails-heads" become the same. So, when observing the state of two such particles, there are only three possible scenarios: heads-heads, tails-tails, and heads-tails.

If we still assume the same probability for each of these three scenarios, we arrive at the conclusion that "the probability of each scenario is one-third." This means that multiple "identical, indistinguishable" objects follow a different statistical law than multiple "distinguishable" objects.

Bose immediately realized this unexpected error might be an "error that wasn't wrong." Based on this, he decided to further investigate the essence of the 1/3 probability differing from the 1/4 probability. After extensive research, Bose wrote a paper titled "Planck's Law and the Hypothesis of Light Quanta." In it, Bose first posited that the classical Maxwell-Boltzmann statistical law was not suitable for microscopic particles, advocating a new statistical method for counting particles.

Einstein supported Bose's hypothesis. In fact, Bose's "error" led to correct results because photons are indeed indistinguishable particles, later collectively termed "bosons." Einstein had vague ideas about this, and Bose's calculations perfectly matched these thoughts. Einstein translated the paper into German and arranged for its publication in the *Physikalische Zeitschrift*. Bose's findings even led Einstein to call a series of papers he wrote "Bose Statistics." Because of Einstein's contributions, it is now known as "Bose-Einstein statistics." Later, the theory of "Bose-Einstein Condensation" at ultra-low temperatures was developed.

3.1.2 Two Identical Particles

In our understanding of the macroscopic world, it seems impossible for two things to be exactly alike. Even in the case of identical twins with the same genes, their individual life experiences, memories, and meals are never completely identical. Therefore, there will always be differences in their physical appearance and neural connections in the brain. Similarly, standard products manufactured in the same factory, such as mobile phones, are not absolutely identical. A closer inspection would reveal distinct abrasions on the components and subtle differences on the glass.

In the macro world, no two things, even if they appear identical, are truly indistinguishable. For example, they cannot occupy the same position at the same time. If we place these two objects side by side, one must be on the left and the other on the right, differentiating them as the object on the left and the object on the right.

However, Bose's hypothesis challenges this notion. The correctness of Bose's "error" stems from the indistinguishability of photons. In quantum mechanics, such indistinguishable and identical particles are known as "identical particles."

Identical particles are those with exactly the same intrinsic properties such as mass, charge, and spin—something impossible in the macro world. According to classical mechanics, even if two particles are identical, their trajectories will differ. Thus, we can distinguish them by tracking these distinct trajectories. However, in the quantum world, which follows the laws of quantum mechanics, particles obey the uncertainty principle and lack fixed trajectories, making them indistinguishable.

The principle of identical particles, sometimes referred to as the indistinguishability of identical particles, is twofold in Planck's view: interchangeability and indistinguishability. The concept of particle identicalness is fundamentally linked to the quantization of particle states. This concept suggests that while classical particles can be distinguished, identical particles lack such distinctiveness. For instance, two iron atoms, even if produced by different methods, would still be considered identical in their ground state under normal conditions. This notion would be hard to accept in classical theory. Hence, many theories in quantum mechanics indeed break our conventional understanding.

The principle of identical particles, one of the foundational formulas of quantum mechanics, cannot be proven, but its validity has been repeatedly verified through exploration and practice. It forms the mathematical system of quantum mechanics, along with measurement formulas, wave function formulas, operator formulas, and the dynamic evolution formulas of microscopic systems.

3.1.3 Behind Quantum Spin

As Bose proposed the indistinguishability of quantum particles, three young physicists, independently of Bose and Einstein, began to explore this notion: Pauli, Fermi, and Dirac. Pauli, only 18 and freshly graduated from high school, had published his first paper on general relativity. Fermi was one of the few physicists adept in both theory and experiment. Dirac, introverted and reticent, was nonetheless undeterred in his research. Under the collective studies of Pauli, Fermi, and Dirac, another class of identical particles, fermions, was successfully introduced.

In 1922, Niels Bohr visited Göttingen, delivering a series of lectures on how quantum theory could explain the arrangement of the periodic table. Despite some progress, Bohr could not address the biggest challenge: why electrons don't accumulate at the lowest energy level. This question troubled Pauli for over three years until, inspired by others' work, he finally resolved it in 1925.

Pauli suggested two assumptions to explain the periodic table: first, besides spatial degrees of freedom, electrons possess a strange degree of freedom, soon verified to be spin. To understand spin, one must first grasp the concept of angular momentum. Commonly exemplified by a figure skater's spin, where the skater spins faster as they pull in their arms, due to the conservation of angular momentum. Simplistically, angular momentum can be thought of as the product of the area swept by the rotation and the speed of rotation, a constant value. In classical physics, the total angular momentum of electrons and atoms is conserved. However, experiments showed that in some cases, part of the system's angular momentum seemed to disappear, a puzzling phenomenon. It was later discovered that electrons themselves possess angular momentum, and the system's "lost" angular momentum was transferred to the electrons, maintaining overall conservation. Since angular momentum is related to rotation, physicists named the electron's angular momentum as spin. It's important to note that despite its name, an electron does not spin like a top.

Furthermore, an electron's spin state has only two degrees of freedom. To understand this concept of electron spin, consider a spinning figure skater as an electron. Regardless of the direction we observe from, we can only see one of two outcomes: either their head is spinning toward us or their feet. No other scenarios are possible. This rough analogy represents the concept of electrons having only two degrees of freedom.

The second assumption was that no two electrons can occupy the same quantum state simultaneously, now known as the Pauli Exclusion Principle. This assumption inspired Fermi and eventually led to the hypothesis of fermions. Fermi had been pondering the distinguishability of electrons since 1924. Bohr-Sommerfeld theory could not explain the spectrum of helium atoms. Fermi speculated the main reason was the indistinguishability of the two electrons in a helium atom, but he struggled to initiate a quantitative discussion until he read Pauli's article.

In 1926, Fermi published two papers describing a new type of quantum gas, with particles being identical and indistinguishable, and each quantum state occupied by only one particle. This was different from the identical particles discussed by Bose and Einstein, a difference arising from electron spin and the resulting symmetry.

Beyond theoretical achievements, Fermi's experimental contributions were unparalleled. He built the first controlled nuclear reactor, ushering humanity into the atomic age and earning the title "Father of the Atomic Bomb." In his honor, element 100, fermium, the renowned Fermi Laboratory in Chicago, and the Fermi Institute at the University of Chicago were named after him. He also collaborated with Chen-Ning Yang to propose the first composite model of fundamental particles. In many areas of quantum physics, Fermi's research was groundbreaking.

3.1.4 Bosons and Fermions

The emergence of two types of identical particles, bosons and fermions, marked a significant step in the advancement of quantum theory.

Bosons are particles with integer spin, such as photons, which have a spin of 1. The wave function of two bosons is symmetric upon exchange, meaning the total wave function remains unchanged when two bosons swap roles. On the other hand, fermions have half-integer spins, like electrons, which have a spin of 1/2.

The wave function of a system composed of two fermions is antisymmetric upon exchange, changing its sign when two fermions swap roles. This antisymmetry is related to the Pauli Exclusion Principle, which all fermions follow. Consequently, no two electrons in an atom can occupy the same quantum state, leading to the layered arrangement of electrons in atoms and the epoch-making Periodic Law.

Simply put, bosons prefer to cohabit in the same state, eagerly crowding into the lowest energy state. For instance, photons, being bosons, can occupy the same energy level, enabling the creation of high-intensity laser beams. Atoms, as composite particles, are a bit more complex. For composite particles, those composed of an odd number of fermions are fermions, while those made of an even number of fermions are bosons.

When bosonic atoms are cooled to near absolute zero under certain conditions, all bosons suddenly "condense" together, exhibiting "superfluid" properties not observed in normal matter. This phenomenon is known as "Bose-Einstein Condensation." In-depth research into this phenomenon could lead to promising breakthroughs like "atomic lasers."

We now know that microscopic particles are divided into two classes: bosons and fermions. Bosons obey Bose-Einstein statistics, allowing multiple bosons to occupy the same quantum state, with symmetric wave functions. Fermions obey Fermi-Dirac statistics, where a quantum state can be occupied by only one fermion at most, and fermionic systems have antisymmetric wave functions.

The calculation of probabilities for indistinguishable identical particles indeed differs from classical statistical methods. As illustrated, the probability of getting two heads (HH) is 1/4 for two classical particles, whereas for bosons like photons, it's 1/3. Fermions, also identical particles, follow the Pauli Exclusion Principle (two electrons cannot occupy the same state). Using the two-coin analogy, if the coins are now "fermionic coins," two fermions can't be in the same state, so the HH and TT possibilities are invalid, leaving only HT. Therefore, for a two-fermion system, the probability of HT is 1, and other states is 0.

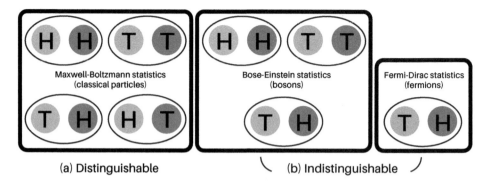

(a) Distinguishable   (b) Indistinguishable

Beyond the difference in their spin properties, bosons and fermions also exhibit other distinctions. Bosons are elastic, allowing them to coexist well in the same space. Fermions, however, form their own space and repel other fermions. In this respect, bosons seem more selfless, while fermions resemble territorial animals. Common bosons include the Higgs boson and photons, which do not follow the Pauli Exclusion Principle and can undergo Bose-Einstein Condensation at low temperatures. Common fermions include neutrons, protons, and electrons, which adhere to the Pauli Exclusion Principle.

3.2 Matrix Mechanics and Uncertainty Principle

While Bose, Einstein, Fermi, and Dirac were developing the concept of particle indistinguishability, Heisenberg and Born were making breakthroughs in another direction of quantum theory, laying the foundations for what Born envisioned as "quantum mechanics." At 20, Heisenberg introduced the concept of half-quantum numbers; by 24, he had broken away from old quantum theory and established matrix mechanics.

3.2.1 Introducing Matrix Operations into the Quantum World

Bohr's theory had successfully salvaged the nuclear model of the atom. Still, it struggled to explain helium atoms or atoms with more nuclear charges. Heisenberg reflected deeply on the root of this failure. He believed the key issue lay in incorporating too many unobservable concepts in experiments, such as "orbit" and "orbital frequency." Heisenberg proposed eliminating these unobservable quantities and instead starting with concepts that had experimental significance. He realized that while orbits (energy levels) were not directly observable, the energy absorbed or emitted during transitions between levels was meaningful. These data could be tabulated in two-dimensional matrixes, which evolved into observable quantities in quantum mechanics capable of specific operations. This marked the introduction of matrixes and their operations into subatomic physics.

In September 1925, Heisenberg published a seminal paper titled "Quantum-Theoretical Reinterpretation of Kinematic and Mechanical Relations." He wrote, "This paper aims to establish a basis for quantum mechanics that will include only the relationships between observable quantities." This work, later refined and systematized by Born, Jordan, and Dirac, signified the birth of matrix mechanics, a direct precursor to modern quantum mechanics.

In matrix mechanics, physical quantities like position and momentum were no longer represented by numbers but by large tables (matrixes). This meant that the product of position and momentum did not equal the product of momentum and position. Born and Jordan even calculated the difference between these two products. Heisenberg's matrix mechanics earned him the 1932 Nobel Prize in Physics and cemented his role as a leading figure in quantum mechanics.

3.2.2 Deriving the Uncertainty Principle from Matrix Mechanics

In April 1926, Heisenberg presented on matrix mechanics at a renowned physics conference, emphasizing that quantum mechanics could be verified through "measurement." Post-conference, Heisenberg realized that physical quantity measurements had an "uncertainty," the "indeterminacy relation." The precision in measuring an electron's position and the precision in measuring its momentum multiplied together equaled a constant, namely half of Planck's constant. Heisenberg published his findings in "The Perceptual Content of Quantum Kinematic and Mechanical Theory."

Heisenberg's Uncertainty Principle formula indicated that the deviations in measurements of momentum and position could not simultaneously be minimized: as one quantity is measured more accurately, the error in the other increases. For instance, precise measurement of position results in significant uncertainty in momentum and vice versa.

To illustrate his principle, Heisenberg devised a thought experiment using a gamma-ray microscope to observe an electron. The microscope's precision was limited by the wavelength of light used—the shorter the wavelength, the higher the precision. However, shorter wavelengths meant higher frequencies and more energetic photons.

Heisenberg argued that using high-energy gamma rays to observe an electron could precisely measure its position. Still, the collision would significantly alter the electron's state of motion, affecting its momentum. Thus, a gamma-ray microscope could accurately determine an electron's position, but its disturbance rendered the momentum measurement inaccurate.

The uncertainty principle, though perplexing, becomes clearer when described mathematically. A quantum system, such as the electron considered by Heisenberg, is described at any moment by a wave function, which only yields the probabilities of the system having certain properties. This probability leads to the impossibility of precisely predicting an electron's position.

Considering the distribution of an electron in space, a measurement might yield the electron's exact location, but measuring a million electrons in the same state would show dispersed locations. This dispersion reflects the probability inherent in the wave function. Similar characteristics are observed in other properties, like momentum.

Mathematical tools called operators are needed to calculate the probabilities of a particle's position and momentum from the wave function. Quantum mechanics features various operators, such as those for position and momentum. When applied to a wave function, these operators, like the position operator, yield the potential locations of an electron and the probability of it being at those locations. Each operator has a set of wave functions called eigenstates. A particle in a position eigenstate has a 100% probability of being at a specific location.

The same applies to other operators. The momentum operator also has eigenstates, with particles in these states having a definite momentum. Mathematically, however, it's evident that a particle cannot simultaneously be in the eigenstates of both momentum and position. Just as 2 + 3 will never equal 27, the mathematical requirements of the operators dictate that momentum and position cannot simultaneously be in eigenstates.

Mathematically, these two mechanical quantities can't have definite values simultaneously. The indeterminacy of quantum physics seems to limit our precision in measuring an electron's position and momentum.

According to the uncertainty principle, nothing is absolutely stationary. If a particle had an absolute velocity of 0, it would have no uncertainty in momentum, necessitating infinite uncertainty in position, meaning it would have to appear everywhere in the universe. In reality, even at absolute zero, particles exhibit slight vibrations.

The uncertainty principle implies that "electron orbits" are meaningless. Electrons don't have a definite position; they appear everywhere outside the nucleus, forming a "cloud." In fact, even the nucleus is a cloud. The reason we can precisely know an object's position and speed in everyday life is due to the smallness of Planck's constant compared to macroscopic scales.

The "Uncertainty Principle" is a significant contribution of Heisenberg to quantum mechanics. With the development of quantum theory, the importance of Heisenberg's "Uncertainty Principle" in the microscopic world became apparent, and a series of simultaneously imprecise physical quantities were discovered. Today, the uncertainty principle is widely applied in high-energy physics, particle physics, computing, biochemistry, philosophy, and economics, directly or indirectly driving progress in these areas.

3.3   Is the World a Game of Chance?

According to Heisenberg's hypothesis, the world would be a game of chance, with all matter in the universe, from atoms to subatomic particles, governed by probability rather than certainty. Quantum mechanics fundamentally suggests that nature is based on randomness, a concept that contradicts our intuitive understanding and has sparked controversy in the field of quantum mechanics.

3.3.1 Schrödinger's Misunderstanding of His Own Equation

Heisenberg's Uncertainty Principle asserts that particles cannot simultaneously have definite positions and corresponding momenta. An electron at any given moment could be located at any point in space, each with different probabilities. In other words, the state of the electron at that moment is a superposition of states at all fixed points, each with a certain probability, termed the electron's quantum "superposition state." Each fixed point is considered an "eigenstate" of the electron's position.

In quantum theory, for example, an electron's spin is interpreted as an intrinsic property of the electron, observable only as either "spin-up" or "spin-down" eigenstates. Thus, a superposition state is a probability-weighted superposition of eigenstates, allowing for an infinite combination of probabilities.

An electron being in a superposition of both "spin-up" and "spin-down" is a fundamental principle in quantum mechanics. Photons also have superposition states, as seen in polarization, where a single photon's electromagnetic field oscillates both vertically and horizontally, thus being in both "vertical" and "horizontal" states.

However, when we measure a particle's state (such as an electron), the superposition state ceases to exist; its spin becomes either "up" or "down." To explain this process, Heisenberg introduced the concept of wave function collapse, where the electron's wave function, initially representing an uncertain position, suddenly collapses to a specific position upon observation.

This is the Copenhagen interpretation, where the wave function is interpreted as a probability cloud. It doesn't reveal the actual state of the electron but shows the likelihood of obtaining a specific result upon measurement. However, this is merely a statistical model, not a reality. It doesn't prove the reality of the wave function.

The Copenhagen interpretation, reflecting what occurs in experiments, doesn't make detailed assumptions about observing quantum systems. Nevertheless, it effectively explains the behavior of electrons, photons, and other quantum systems.

However, the Copenhagen interpretation and the concept of quantum superposition greatly contradict everyday experience, causing concern for Schrödinger. To challenge the Copenhagen interpretation of quantum mechanics, Schrödinger proposed a thought experiment involving a cat, known today as "Schrödinger's cat."

Schrödinger imagined a cat enclosed in a box with poisonous gas triggered by a radioactive atom. At a certain moment, the atom might decay, emitting radiation. The detector would detect this and break the poison bottle, killing the cat.

In quantum mechanics, the decay of a radioactive atom is random. From the outside, no observer can tell if the atom has decayed. According to the Copenhagen interpretation, before an atom (quantum) is observed, it is in a superposition state of both decayed and undecayed. The detector, poison bottle, and cat are in the same state. Thus, the cat is in a superposition of being both dead and alive.

Since the box is isolated from all quantum interactions, the only way to determine whether the atom has decayed and killed the cat is to open the box. The Copenhagen interpretation suggests that upon opening the box, the wave function collapses, and the cat suddenly shifts to a definite state: either dead or alive. But the problem is, there's no difference between the inside of the box and the outside world. In the outside world, we never observe a cat in a superposition state; a cat is either dead or alive, not both.

Although real cats cannot be dead and alive, the behavior of electrons (or atoms) is such. This experiment put Schrödinger again in opposition to the theory he helped establish, leading some physicists to jest, "Schrödinger didn't understand Schrödinger's equation."

3.3.2 Searching for Schrödinger's Cat

Schrödinger attempted to refute the Copenhagen interpretation with his "both dead and alive" cat paradox, pointing out a perceived flaw. While microscopic quantum systems can follow the principle of superposition, macroscopic systems cannot. By linking the atomic elements of the microscopic system with a macroscopic cat, Schrödinger highlighted the inapplicability of the Copenhagen interpretation to macroscopic states. After all, in the formalism of quantum theory, there's ample reason to require any "observable" measurement to be an eigenfunction.

The Copenhagen interpretation suggests that the measurement process somehow decomposes the complex, superposed wave function into a single-component eigenfunction. If Schrödinger's equation allowed wave functions to behave this way, everything would be fine, but that's not true. The instantaneous collapse of the wave function doesn't emerge from Schrödinger's mathematics; rather, the Copenhagen interpretation supplements the theory.

So, if the fundamental quantum building blocks of the world can exist in a superposed state, why does the universe appear classical? Many physicists have conducted experiments to prove that the behavior of electrons and atoms aligns with quantum mechanics. But the key question theorists want to answer is: can the cat observe its state? Their conclusion aligns with Schrödinger's logic. If the cat observes its state, the box contains a superposition of a dead cat that committed suicide by observation and a living cat that observes itself to be alive, until the actual observer opens the box.

The measurement process isn't the ideal operation assumed by the Copenhagen interpretation. Wave function collapse into a single eigenfunction describes the input and output of the measurement process. However, when we conduct actual measurements, from a quantum perspective, what we're doing is incredibly complex, and realistically modeling it is obviously impossible. For instance, to measure an electron's spin, it interacts with a suitable device with a pointer that can move to "up" or "down" positions. This device produces a state, and only one state. We don't see the pointer in a superposed position of up and down.

This is, in fact, how the classical world operates. Below the classical world lies a quantum one. Replace the cat with a spinning device; it, indeed, should exist in a superposed state. This device, treated as a quantum system, is extremely complex. It contains countless particles. In a sense, the measurement results come from the interaction of a single electron with these numerous particles, making it difficult for physicists to analyze a real measurement process using Schrödinger's equation.

Currently, we have some understanding of the quantum world. For example, a beam of light striking a mirror is considered in the classical world to reflect at an angle equal to the angle of incidence. Physicist Richard Feynman, in his book on quantum electrodynamics, explains that this isn't what happens in the quantum world. Light is actually a beam of photons, each capable of reflecting anywhere.

However, the superposition of all possible actions a photon might take results in Snell's law. If all quantum states of an optical system are superposed, the classical result emerges, with light traveling the shortest path.

This example clearly demonstrates that the superposition of all possibilities—in this optical framework—creates the classical world. The most important feature isn't the geometric details of the light path but that it can only produce one world at the classical level. In the quantum details of a single photon, we can observe everything superposed, such as eigenfunctions. But at the human scale, all of this cancels out, creating a classical world.

Another part of this explanation is called decoherence. Quantum waves have phases and amplitudes. Phase is critical for any superposition. If you take two superposed states, change the phase of one, and then add them together, you can end up with something entirely different. If you do the same with many components and recombine the waves, they can be almost anything. The loss of phase information destroys Schrödinger's cat-like superpositions. We not only can't discern whether it's dead or alive; we can't even tell it's a cat.

When quantum waves no longer have coherent phase relationships, they behave more classically, and superposition loses meaning. The cause of their decoherence is interactions with surrounding particles, which is likely the reason instruments measuring electron spin get a specific result.

Both methods lead to the same conclusion: if we observe a very complex quantum system containing countless particles from a human perspective, we see classical physics. Special experimental methods and devices might preserve some quantum effects, but as we return to larger scales, general quantum systems quickly cease to display quantum effects.

This is one way to explain the fate of the cat. The experiment can produce a superposed cat if the box is completely unaffected by quantum decoherence, but such a box does not exist.

3.3.3 Possibility of Parallel Universes?

The conundrum of the quantum world, exemplified by "Schrödinger's cat," led to another interpretation: the theory of parallel universes. This concept was integrated into various quantum phenomena in the sci-fi epic *Interstellar*, directed by Christopher Nolan.

In 1957, Hugh Everett III proposed the many-worlds interpretation of quantum mechanics. Everett didn't regard observation as a special process. In this interpretation, both the dead and alive states of the cat continue to exist after the box is opened, but they become decoherent from each other. In other words, upon opening the box, the observer and the cat split into two branches: one observing a dead cat and the other a live cat. However, since the dead and alive states are decoherent, they cannot effectively exchange information or interact. This state is known as quantum superposition, associated with a random subatomic event that might or might not occur.

Everett viewed this system as the entire universe. Everything interacts with everything else, and only the universe is truly isolated. He found that if we take this step, the problem of the cat, and the contradiction between quantum and classical realities, become easily resolvable. The quantum wave function of the universe is not a pure eigenfunction but a superposition of all possible eigenfunctions. While we can't calculate these things, we can reason about them. Essentially, from the perspective of quantum mechanics, we're portraying the universe as a combination of everything the universe could do.

As a result, the cat's wave function doesn't need to collapse to yield a classical observation. It can remain entirely unchanged, not violating Schrödinger's equation. Instead, there are two coexisting universes. In one, the cat dies in the experiment; in the other, it lives. When you open the box, there are two of you and two boxes. A unique classical world emerges in some way from the superposition of quantum possibilities, replaced by a vast array of classical worlds, each corresponding to a quantum possibility.

This is the many-worlds interpretation of quantum mechanics. Subsequently, some hypothesized that considering quantum superposition, even after opening the box, the cat inside might not be the same as before, possibly having switched with an identical cat from a parallel universe. In other words, every probabilistic event might generate a parallel universe equivalent to its probability. In these parallel universes, an identical "you" exists but with potentially entirely different personal backgrounds and information. Many physicists have accepted the many-worlds interpretation. Schrödinger's cat is indeed both alive and dead. This is the mathematical result. It's not just an interpretation or a computational method. It's as real as you and me.

The universe is likely a highly complex superposition of various states. If you believe quantum mechanics is fundamentally correct, it must be. However, Stephen

Hawking refuted the many-worlds interpretation. In 1983, physicist Stephen Hawking stated that the many-worlds interpretation is "trivially true" in this sense. But this doesn't imply the existence of a superposed universe. Hawking believed, "What people do is merely calculate conditional probabilities—in other words, the probability of A happening given B. I think that's all there is to the many-worlds interpretation."

A CAT'S MISSION

4.1 The Reconstruction of Computing

Despite Schrödinger's opposition, the concept of quantum superposition has been widely accepted since the emergence of quantum computing in the 1980s. Quantum computers are a quintessential application of quantum superposition states.

In 1981, renowned physicist Richard Feynman observed the difficulties conventional computers encountered, based on the Turing model, in simulating quantum mechanical systems. This led to the idea of using classical computers to simulate quantum systems. When quantum physics intersected with computing in 1985, the concept of a universal quantum computer was finally born. Since then, quantum mechanics has rapidly transformed into a tangible social technology, and humanity's progress in developing and applying quantum computers has accelerated. Today, quantum computing is no longer a distant reality.

4.1.1 From Classical to Quantum Computing

Classic electronic computing in conventional computers utilizes the laws of classical electromagnetism to manipulate physical systems. In contrast, quantum computing manipulates physical systems using the principles of quantum mechanics, handling quantum bits (qubits).

In classical computers, classical bits have two states: 0 and 1, akin to the two sides of a coin, with heads representing 0 and tails representing 1. After logical gate operations, the outcome is either 0 or 1, not simultaneously. Classical computers operate through digital logic, processing strings of digits or bits as input and output.

In contrast, quantum computers allow qubits to be both 0 and 1 simultaneously. Not only can 0 and 1 coexist in quantum superposition, but their proportions can also be adjusted during initialization. This property, enabling multiple states at once, exponentially enhances information processing speed. It can be visualized as a spinning coin, where, at high speeds, both heads and tails appear simultaneously—a state known as "quantum superposition" in quantum mechanics. This characteristic theoretically enables quantum computers to surpass classical computers several times, even hundreds or thousands, in certain applications.

While a 2-bit register in a classical computer can store only one binary number at a time, a 2-qubit register in a quantum computer can hold all four states simultaneously. When the number of qubits is "n," a quantum processor operating on "n" qubits is equivalent to executing 2^n operations on classical bits, significantly speeding up quantum computing.

Consider a calculator composed of 3 qubits. In a classical 3-bit system, binary 101 plus binary 010 equals 111, i.e., decimal 5 + 2 = 7. However, in a 3-qubit system, each qubit is a superposition of 0 and 1, simultaneously representing decimal numbers 0 to 7. Upon inputting 2 (binary 010) and issuing a computation command, all 8 numbers begin processing, each adding 2 and yielding 8 results simultaneously. Thus, a classical 3-bit system computes one result at a time, whereas a quantum system computes 8 results at once, effectively increasing the computation speed.

Furthermore, quantum mechanics dictate that energy is quantized at the microscopic level, akin to discovering a flight of stairs under a magnifying glass examining an inclined plane. Quantum isn't a particle but denotes the phenomenon of energy discretization in the microscopic world. Quantum systems collapse into classical states after "measurement." After computation, a classical computer outputs one definite number, while a quantum computer outputs 8 indeterminate numbers. However, the results of quantum computation cannot be fully outputted; once outputted, the quantum superposition state collapses into one of the 8 values, irretrievably losing the others.

This collapse, known as "decoherence" in quantum computing, brings quantum systems back to classical states, collapsing superpositions to fixed eigenstates and ending particle entanglement. If decoherence occurs during computation, it affects the results, causing errors in quantum computing.

Nonetheless, quantum computing demonstrates unprecedented advantages. Unlike classical computers' linear growth, quantum computing power exponentially increases with the number of qubits. This capability grants quantum computers the extraordinary ability to process numerous results simultaneously.

In an unobserved superposition state, "n" qubits can contain information equivalent to 2^n classical bits. Thus, 4 qubits are equivalent to 16 classical bits, seemingly a minor improvement. However, 16 qubits correspond to 65,536 classical bits, and 300 qubits represent more states than the estimated total atoms in the universe—a colossal number. This exponential effect is why quantum computers are so highly anticipated. Simply put, quantum computers are fast and secure.

For example, proteins, composed of long chains of amino acids, become useful biological machines when folded into complex shapes. Deciphering protein folding methods is significant for biology and medicine.

A classic supercomputer might brute-force protein folding, examining various potential chemical chain bends with numerous processors before concluding. However, as protein sequences grow longer and more complex, supercomputers grind to a halt. A chain of 100 amino acids, theoretically foldable in trillions of ways, exceeds the working memory of any computer to process all possible folding combinations.

Quantum computing, however, offers a novel approach to this complex problem, such as creating multidimensional spaces to identify correlations between individual data points in these spaces.

Quantum computing utilizes the superposition states of qubits to represent data points in multidimensional spaces. This means a qubit can simultaneously represent multiple possible values, and multiple qubits together form a high-dimensional vector space. In protein folding problems, we seek the relationships and interactions among amino acids, which constitute the patterns of protein folding.

Traditional classical methods might try numerous possibilities, but quantum computing can more efficiently find these correlations and patterns in multidimensional spaces. With expanding quantum hardware scales and algorithmic advancements, they can tackle protein folding problems too complex for any supercomputer, significantly shortening breakthroughs in relevant fields.

4.1.2 Surpassing Classical Computing

The concept of "quantum supremacy," or "quantum superiority," is achieved when quantum computing surpasses the capabilities of the strongest existing classical computers in a particular problem. This concept was introduced in 2011 by American theoretical physicist John Preskill. It is widely believed that achieving quantum supremacy marks the transition of quantum computing from theoretical experimentation to general utility.

In 2019, Google announced the achievement of "quantum supremacy," propelling quantum computing into public attention and stirring a wave of interest in the field.

According to Google's publication, their quantum computer, named "Sycamore," addressed a problem roughly akin to "verifying whether a quantum random number generator is truly random." The "Sycamore" consists of a 53-qubit chip and can sample a quantum circuit a million times in just 200 seconds. In contrast, the world's largest supercomputer, Summit, would require 10,000 years to perform the same amount of computation. If these results represent the best performance of both parties, it signifies a decisive advantage of quantum computing over super-computing. Therefore, this work is considered the first experimental verification of quantum superiority in human history and has been hailed as a milestone in the history of quantum computing by *Nature*.

In 2020, a Chinese team announced the emergence of the "Jiuzhang" quantum computer, challenging Google's "quantum supremacy" and achieving global leadership in computational power. "Jiuzhang," a quantum computer with 76 photonic qubits and 100 modes, performed "Gaussian Boson Sampling" a hundredtrillion times faster than the world's fastest supercomputer, "Fugaku." A quantum computer built using photons outperformed the fastest classical supercomputer in computational speed for the first time. It was also a hundred billion times faster than Google's 53-qubit superconducting qubit quantum computer prototype "Sycamore" launched in 2019. This breakthrough made China the second country to achieve "quantum supremacy" and pushed quantum computing research to the next milestone.

Many scientists believe that quantum computers will far surpass any classical computer in specific tasks due to quantum superposition. However, the path to achieving quantum supremacy remains challenging and is linked to the conditions for achieving it.

Scientists speculate that quantum supremacy could be realized when a certain number of precisely manipulated qubits is surpassed. This includes two key points: the number of qubits manipulated and the precision of these qubits. Quantum computing superiority can only be achieved when both conditions are met.

However, whether it is Google's "Sycamore," which achieved quantum supremacy with 54 qubits, or the "Jiuzhang" quantum computing prototype built with

76 photons, scientists face increasing technical challenges in quantum computing accuracy as they manipulate a growing number of qubits.

One reason is that, unlike classical bits, qubits are susceptible to external disturbances and noise, including thermal noise and electromagnetic interference. These interferences can cause errors in qubits, reducing computational accuracy. As the number of qubits increases, the impact of noise and errors also grows, posing a serious challenge to building large-scale quantum computers. In large systems, accuracy issues may become more prominent as errors may propagate and interact among different qubits.

Another aspect is the duration of coherence time for qubits, the time length they can maintain a quantum state. The longer a qubit maintains its superposition state (representing both 1 and 0 simultaneously), the more program steps it can process, and thus the more complex computations it can perform. When qubits lose coherence, information is lost. Therefore, quantum computing technology faces challenges in controlling and reading qubits. After achieving high fidelity in reading and controlling, operations for quantum error correction on the quantum system are required. Currently, no quantum circuit is 100% reliable (they all introduce errors), and the errors increase with the time required to complete computations and the number of qubits involved.

4.1.3 Will Quantum Computing Replace Classical Computing?

Pursuing quantum supremacy has always been a pinnacle of quantum computing, demonstrating its unparalleled advantages. Quantum computing holds a vast potential for future applications, but does this mean quantum computers will replace classical computers? The answer is no.

For instance, Google's "Sycamore" quantum computer's superiority relies on its sample size. While it holds an absolute advantage over a supercomputer when collecting 1 million samples, the situation changes with 10 billion samples. In this case, a classical computer would need only 2 days, while "Sycamore" would require 20 days, losing its edge.

Moreover, current quantum computers excel only in specific tasks. Google's quantum computer, for example, was tailored for "Random Circuit Sampling." The selection of such specific tasks is carefully considered to suit the quantum system and be challenging for classical computation.

This means quantum computers don't surpass classical computers in all areas, only in certain problems where efficient quantum algorithms are designed. Without suitable quantum algorithms, they do not hold an advantage. Meanwhile, classical computation algorithms and hardware continue to improve, and the potential of supercomputing projects cannot be underestimated. However, traditional classical computing faces limitations and challenges in existing physical theories and material properties. Hyperdimensional computing might be a direction for breakthroughs in classical computing.

It is almost certain that for a considerable future, classical and quantum computers will coexist, each handling different computational domains. With the maturation of quantum computing technology, future computers might include classical and quantum components, each addressing tasks suited to their strengths.

For example, quantum computing would be valuable in handling complex problems involving numerous input variables and intricate algorithms. Such computations would be time-consuming on classical computers. Quantum computers could narrow the range of potential input variables and solution approaches. After this step, the classical computer could directly produce the answer using the input range provided by the quantum computer.

However, in the long term, with global development and deployment, quantum computing may ultimately eliminate time barriers, and costs will also decrease. But until a universally functional quantum computer, similar to traditional computers, is developed, quantum computing will still require an extended exploration period.

4.2 Creating Quantum Algorithms for Quantum Computing

Just like classical computing, quantum computing also requires specific algorithms. Quantum algorithms, designed for high-speed quantum computers, not only fulfill the immense potential of quantum computers but also open new possibilities for quantum artificial intelligence (QAI).

4.2.1 Milestones in Quantum Algorithms

In 1985, David Deutsch, a professor at the University of Oxford, introduced the quantum Turing machine model and designed the first quantum algorithm, the Deutsch algorithm. In 1992, Deutsch and Richard Jozsa from the University of Cambridge expanded the early Deutsch algorithm to n quantum bits (qubits). This was the first algorithm to utilize quantum properties, specifically for quantum computers, marking the beginning of quantum algorithms.

The Deutsch-Jozsa algorithm also demonstrated that quantum computers could solve certain problems more quickly and efficiently than classical computers, highlighting the enormous potential of quantum computers.

However, these quantum algorithms remained theoretical due to the time's limited technological and engineering capabilities and an incomplete understanding of quantum properties by theoretical physicists. It wasn't until the 1990s that quantum algorithms began moving from theory to practical application. Three milestone algorithms emerged in quantum algorithm research: Shor's, Grover's, and the HHL algorithm.

Shor's Algorithm

In 1994, Peter Shor of Bell Labs developed a quantum algorithm that could factor large integers into prime numbers in a feasibly short time using quantum computers' inherent parallel computing ability. Known as the quantum factoring algorithm, Shor's algorithm could potentially crack RSA encryption.

RSA encryption, introduced in 1977 by Ron Rivest, Adi Shamir, and Leonard Adleman, is based on the fact that multiplying two primes is easy, but factoring their product back into primes is hard. For a classical computer, cracking a high-bit RSA code is virtually impossible. A machine performing 10^{12} operations per second would take 150,000 years to break a 300-bit RSA code. However, Shor's algorithm can quickly find the prime factors of an integer using a quantum computer, exponentially faster than the fastest classical factoring algorithm.

A 2018 report by the National Academy of Sciences, Engineering, and Medicine predicted that a quantum computer running Shor's algorithm could break a 1,024-bit RSA encryption in a day. For a 300-bit code, it's a matter of seconds. Peter Shor received the Gödel Prize in 1999 for his work.

Grover's Algorithm

In 1996, Lov Grover of Bell Labs proposed the Grover quantum search algorithm, which is recognized as the second major algorithm after Shor's. Grover's algorithm quickly finds a specific item from a large, unsorted set.

For example, choosing the shortest driving route from work to home during rush hour. Using a classical computer, each possible route is calculated individually, ultimately finding the shortest. But with Grover's algorithm, a quantum computer can search more efficiently. The algorithm uses quantum superposition to handle multiple possible routes simultaneously. With N routes, Grover's algorithm needs about $\sqrt{N}$ searches. For 1 million routes, the difference is between 1 million and 1,000 searches.

Moreover, before reading the results, Grover's algorithm repeats certain operations to increase the probability of the output equaling the target to nearly 1. Thus, it reduces error rates before measurement.

HHL Algorithm

In 2009, Aram Harrow, Avinatan Hassidim, and Seth Lloyd from MIT developed the HHL algorithm, which is primarily used for solving systems of linear equations. Classic computers usually need polynomial time for this task, but the HHL algorithm can solve it exponentially faster in certain cases.

The HHL algorithm encodes the coefficient matrix A of a linear system $Ax = b$ into a quantum state, then operates on this state to find the solution vector x. Its exponential acceleration makes it powerful in fields like machine learning and data fitting, where large-scale linear systems are common.

By introducing quantum computing into these problems, computational efficiency is significantly enhanced, making it feasible to handle large data sets and complex models.

4.2.2 Quantum Algorithms Today

Shor's, Grover's, and HHL algorithms represent universal quantum algorithms. Specialized quantum algorithms have also flourished alongside their development.

Since 2009, companies like Google and IBM have focused on scaling quantum computers for engineering applications. Starting with two qubits, they gradually increased to dozens. Realizing the challenges of achieving large-scale, Turing-complete quantum computers, many scientists shifted to non-Turing-complete, specialized quantum architectures. These specialized architectures, not relying on logic gates, are more practical and can solve specific problems in specialized fields.

This period saw the emergence of numerous specialized quantum algorithms, including optimization algorithms like the Variational Quantum Eigensolver and the Quantum Approximation Optimization Algorithm, and sampling algorithms like Boson Sampling and Quantum Walk. Stanford University's Coherent Ising Machine (CIM) and quantum annealing algorithms are represented by D-Wave.

Quantum Annealing Algorithm

Quantum annealing is an alternative to circuit-based algorithms, as it's not constructed from gates. "Annealing" is a metallurgical process involving heating metal and then cooling it at a controlled rate. The goal is to reduce hardness and improve machinability. "Quantum annealing" addresses non-optimal solutions in combinatorial optimization and other mathematical calculations.

Quantum annealing operates through superconducting circuits, CIM implementation of laser pulses, and coherent quantum computing based on simulated annealing (SA). It starts with a quantum superposition of a physical system's possible states (candidate states) and evolves according to the time-dependent Schrödinger equation. Quantum tunneling occurs between different states due to the time-dependent strength of the transverse field, allowing quantum parallelism. When the transverse field is eventually turned off, the system is expected to have solved the original optimization problem or the ground state of the corresponding classical Ising Model. In optimization problems, quantum annealing uses quantum physics to find the lowest energy state, equivalent to its elements' best or near-optimal combination.

Quantum Algorithms in Artificial Intelligence (AI)

Quantum algorithms have also entered the field of AI. Their principles, like superposition and entanglement, are well-suited for solving core optimization problems in AI and machine learning. Since 2018, companies like Google have invested in quantum AI, particularly in areas combining quantum computing with deep learning.

Google's 2020 introduction of the Tensorflow Quantum (TFQ) framework is a notable achievement. TFQ is an open-source library for quantum-classical hybrid machine learning, enabling developers to design, train, and test hybrid quantum-classical models. It can simulate quantum processor algorithms and run quantum parts of these models on real quantum processors. TFQ is used for quantum classification, quantum control, and quantum approximation optimization.

The scope of quantum AI research includes Quantum Convolutional Neural Networks, Quantum Natural Language Processing (QNLP), Quantum Generative Models, and more. Institutions like Stanford University are researching CIM Quantum Neurons.

However, despite the promising prospects of quantum algorithms, their implementation still needs to be improved by the lack of suitable quantum hardware. These algorithms require corresponding quantum computers with a sufficient number of qubits and enough power, which are currently not widely available.

4.3 Pursuing Quantum Computing

With the evolution of quantum algorithms, one of the key challenges for scientists has been building a real quantum computer to run these algorithms.

4.3.1 How to Build a Quantum Computer?

In 2000, physicist DiVincenzo proposed five criteria, suggesting that only a physical system meeting these standards could feasibly construct a quantum computer:

1. Definable quantum bits (qubits). Qubits are the basic units of a quantum computer, akin to bits in a classical computer. However, qubits can represent not just states 0 and 1 but also superpositions of these states and any linear combination thereof. This means qubits can process and store more information than classical bits. Another key feature of qubits is quantum entanglement. When two or more qubits become entangled, they exhibit a strange correlation even when spatially distant. Precise control and manipulation of qubits, including transitions between superposition and entangled states and performing various quantum gate operations, are crucial. Definable qubits are thus the first step in building a quantum computer.

2. Sufficient coherence time for qubits. Coherence time measures the stability and operability of qubits. In quantum computing, it indicates the duration a qubit can maintain a superposition state without interference. Environmental factors like thermal noise and radiation can cause decoherence, shortening this time and disrupting the superposition state. Sufficient coherence time is vital for the functionality of quantum computers, as it determines the speed and capability of quantum gate operations necessary for computations.

3. Qubit initialization. This involves setting the state of a qubit to a specific 0 or 1 to start quantum computing. Due to the superposition property of qubits, initialization in quantum computing is more complex than in classical computing. The initialization process impacts the accuracy and repeatability of quantum computing.

4. Implementation of a universal set of quantum gates. Like logical gates in classical computing (AND, OR, NOT, etc.), quantum gates perform specific operations based on quantum mechanics principles. A universal set of quantum gates allows for the construction of any quantum algorithm, ensuring the programmability of quantum computing. These gates include Hadamard, CNOT, phase gates, etc., enabling a range of operations from creating superposition and entangled states to quantum error correction.

5. Readout of qubits. The final step in quantum computing involves mapping the state of qubits, typically in superposition, to classical bits, i.e., performing a readout. This process usually involves measuring the qubits, which causes them to collapse into a definite state and yields the measurement result. This result represents the output of the computation, translating the quantum information into understandable classical information.

4.3.2 Ion Trap Quantum Computing

Based on the five criteria proposed by DiVincenzo, various quantum systems have been envisioned as foundational architectures for quantum computers, including polarized photons, cavity quantum electrodynamics, ion traps, and NMR. Among these, ion traps and superconducting systems have emerged as frontrunners, considering factors like scalability and control precision.

Ion traps were among the first physical systems attempted for quantum computing. The theoretical approach to quantum computing using ion traps was initially proposed in 1994 by European physicists Cirac and Zoller, and the same year, the NIST in the United States began experimental research in this direction. Ion traps have been used since the late 1950s to improve the precision of spectroscopic measurements.

The working principle of ion traps is straightforward: they use the interaction between charge and magnetic fields to confine the motion of charged particles, thus achieving control over qubits. This control is exact, making ion trap technology excel in stability. Professor Jungsang Kim from Duke University stated, "Trapped ions can generate very stable qubits. They provide stable and well-isolated quantum systems."

Significant attention has been given to ion trap technology in the United States. Chris Monroe, a key figure in quantum computing at the University of Maryland, has been a faithful explorer of the ion trap quantum computer route. In 2016, Chris Monroe and Jungsang Kim founded the quantum computing company IonQ.

On December 11, 2018, IonQ announced two new ion trap quantum computers, boasting 160 storage qubits and 79 operational qubits. In May 2023, IonQ declared that its latest flagship quantum system, the IonQ Aria series, was officially available on the AWS quantum computing cloud platform Amazon Bracket. With 25 algorithmic qubits, it is one of the world's most powerful commercial quantum computers.

IonQ currently employs trapped ion qubits, involving technology such as laser-stimulated ion photon emission, entanglement of photons with ions, and transfer of entangled photons to another ion trap to entangle two ions. The advantage of the IonQ method is that ions can easily interact with each other, whereas achieving similar effects in quantum technology requires "selecting" the appropriate ions and interacting them with lasers.

Another major ion trap quantum computing giant, Quantinuum, a subsidiary of Honeywell, also launched its second-generation quantum computer, H2, in May 2023. It used H2 to find a long-sought mysterious particle—non-Abelian anyons, marking a crucial step toward building a fault-tolerant quantum computer.

In addition to IonQ and Quantinuum, the Austrian company AQT also introduced a new architecture. AQT's 19-inch rack consists of an optical frame and a "trap" frame, including optical systems, communication and readout systems, amplifiers and electronic equipment, optical fiber routing and switches, and other core modules. The optical frame mainly includes light generation, exchange and routing modules, and related electronic devices, including coherent radiofrequency (RF) and digital signal generation modules. The "trap" frame accommodates the main trap module, related driving electronic devices, and communication and remote-control hubs.

Furthermore, QDOOR's cutting-edge quantum computing measurement and control system, Qusoul, features China's first ARTIQ (Advanced Real-Time Infrastructure for Quantum Physics) architecture with independent intellectual property rights. Positioned at the forefront of quantum information experiments, this advanced control and data acquisition system is one of the most advanced and widely used quantum measurement and control systems globally.

Despite the technical maturity of the ion trap approach, its limited scalability hampers its development toward practical quantum computers. Scalability refers to the system's capacity to add more qubits, a crucial step toward practical quantum computing applications.

4.3.3 Superconducting Quantum Computing

Currently, the scientific community recognizes superconducting technology as the most scalable solution for quantum computing. Superconductivity is when certain materials exhibit zero electrical resistance and complete diamagnetism when cooled to a certain temperature. The core component of a superconducting quantum computer is a superconducting electronic device called the Josephson junction. This junction is a "superconductor–insulator–superconductor" three-layer structure with two superconductors connected through a nanoscale insulator layer.

Since the 1980s, scientists have observed macroscopic quantum phenomena such as energy level quantization and quantum tunneling in superconducting Josephson circuits. Compared to natural quantum systems like atoms and photons, the energy level structure of superconducting qubits based on the Josephson junction can be customized by circuit design and controlled with external electromagnetic signals.

Superconducting qubits, being micron-scale in size and thus a thousand times larger than typical quantum systems, can be fabricated using many low-temperature microelectronics device technologies. Extremely low temperatures are necessary because the photon energy used in Josephson quantum circuits is five orders of magnitude smaller than that of visible light. To maintain the coherence of such low-energy quantum states, environmental noise must be significantly lower than this energy level difference. Therefore, superconducting quantum computers must have dilution refrigerators to operate under extremely low temperatures.

In this technological path, IBM in the United States is leading global developments. Current trends indicate that other superconducting quantum computing companies, including Google, will unlikely surpass IBM in the short term. IBM represents the US international standing in superconducting quantum computing. IBM announced the 433-qubit Osprey, which leads in the number of qubits and offers flexibility in signal routing and device layout through its multi-layer wiring. Separating the wires and components required for readout and control into separate layers helps protect the fragile qubits from damage and allows the processor to incorporate more qubits.

In China, Alibaba has invested in the team of Academician Pan Jianwei, establishing the Chinese Academy of Sciences—Alibaba Quantum Computing Laboratory at the Shanghai Research Institute of the University of Science and Technology of China, focusing on the superconducting approach.

The team led by Academician Pan Jianwei in China has a leading position in the photonic quantum approach. They use single photons as qubits and perform quantum computing through complex optical systems. If photons are not absorbed or scattered, their coherence can be maintained for a long time. However, the photonic quantum approach faces challenges in scalability due to limitations in photon linewidth and integrated optical circuits.

This is why, despite the extreme fragility of coherence in superconducting systems, they remain the primary technological route—because currently, only superconducting systems can meet the scalability requirements of quantum computers.

This essay collection is unique because international experts wrote most articles based on their observations and research. Its purpose is to be a reference for researchers, and anyone interested in learning about China.

4.3.4 Multiple Technological Approaches

Beyond ion traps and superconducting quantum computing systems, various other quantum technologies are flourishing, including photonic quantum, neutral atom, quantum dot, topological quantum, NV centers in diamond, NMR, nuclear electric resonance, spin waves, electrons in helium, and more.

Around these diverse technological approaches, nearly 250 companies worldwide are vying for quantum hardware and software. Current hardware efforts primarily focus on increasing the number of qubits, connectivity, and quality, including improved coherence times and gate fidelities.

Photonic Quantum Computing

In photonic quantum computing, Xanadu, a photon quantum computing company, successfully demonstrated quantum superiority in Gaussian Boson Sampling experiments using its latest programmable photon quantum computer, Borealis, in June 2022. Xanadu's next goal is to build a fault-tolerant and error-correcting quantum computer scalable to one million qubits.

QuiX Quantum, a Dutch photonic quantum computing company, launched a new 20-qumode processor in March 2022. This continuous-variable (CV) photonic quantum processor contrasts with PsiQuantum's approach using discrete photonic qubits.

In entangling photon numbers, the Max Planck Institute for Quantum Optics in the United States successfully entangled 14 photons definitively and effectively, setting a new world record.

In March 2022, a team from Peking University in China made a breakthrough in quantum computing by developing a high-dimensional quantum computing chip. They achieved high-dimensional quantum state initialization, manipulation, and measurement on a large-scale integrated silicon-based photonic quantum chip, demonstrating significant advantages of high-dimensional quantum computing over binary qubit encoding regarding computational power, precision, and speed. This achievement could accelerate the development of large-scale photonic quantum computers.

Neutral Atom Quantum Computing

A major advantage of neutral atom quantum computing technology is combining various optical tweezers with accompanying atoms, some of which can be quickly repositioned. This method has been used to build arrays of over 200 neutral atoms using optical tweezer technology, rapidly integrating new and existing techniques to transform these atoms into fully functional quantum computers. This optical tweezer type is more flexible than other platforms like superconductors, as it can interact with a wider range of atoms. In contrast, in superconductors, each qubit can only interact with its direct neighbors on the chip.

In March 2022, a team from the University of Chicago in the United States achieved a record-breaking 512 qubits using a neutral atom system in the lab. In May 2023, Atom Computing researchers reported the latest coherence time record on their 100+ qubit neutral atom quantum computer Phoenix—40 ± 7 seconds, a hundred thousand times the previous figure, marking the longest coherence time on a commercial neutral atom platform. In August, Japan's National Institute of Natural Sciences executed the world's fastest two-qubit gate in just 6.5 nanoseconds. In September, French neutral atom quantum computing company Pasqal announced the launch of a 324-atom quantum processor, the largest globally in terms of qubit scale until November 2022.

Topological Quantum Computing

In quantum computing, we use qubits as the basic unit of information. Unlike classical bits, qubits can simultaneously be in superpositions of multiple states, a peculiar property of quantum mechanics. However, qubits are extremely fragile and susceptible to external environmental disturbances, potentially leading to information loss or errors. This issue becomes especially apparent when increasing the number of qubits, as the chances for interactions and entanglements also increase, raising the likelihood of errors. Topological qubits are a good solution to this problem, as they can be combined into a fixed structure less affected by external disturbances, thus avoiding information loss issues.

Regarding topological qubits, the most researched particle is the Majorana fermion, a predicted special particle identical to its antiparticle. However, these particles have not been observed in nature so far. Thus, scientists are striving to create a type of anyon called Majorana zero modes, different from fundamental particles in nature, to be generated in mixed materials.

A key feature of topological qubits is their ground state's long-range entanglement, a special quantum entanglement not easily observable with traditional experimental methods. Based on this, the Microsoft Azure Quantum team in 2022 proposed a method called the "topological gap protocol" as a standard for deter-mining topological phases through quantum transport measurements to measure the topological phase. If the protocol is achievable, it proves the existence of a topological gap. They designed a device with a topological superconducting wire, its ends hosting Majorana zero modes, with real fermionic operators at each end of the wire. The Microsoft team measured the device's topological gap of over 30 μeV, eliminating the biggest obstacle to creating topological qubits.

Topological qubits offer a potential solution to issues faced by traditional qu-bits, providing a more stable and reliable foundation for future quantum comput-ers.

Since Richard Feynman proposed the idea of quantum computers nearly forty years ago, from fundamental theory to breakthrough experimental progress, no truly practical quantum computer has emerged. However, quantum computers are increasingly becoming a reality, gradually stepping into our lives.

4.4 Where Is Quantum Computing Heading?

In 1994, Bell Labs demonstrated that quantum computers could perform loga-rithmic operations far faster than traditional computers, marking the first suc-cessful experiment since the quantum computing theory was proposed. Since then, the feasibility of quantum computers has been recognized, and over the past two decades, substantial capital has flowed into the field, advancing quantum computers from the "laboratory stage" to the "engineering application stage."

4.4.1 Three Phases of Quantum Computing

The computational power of quantum computers grows exponentially with the number of qubits. Therefore, the core task of quantum computing research is the coherent manipulation of multiple qubits. The international academic community recognizes the following development phases for quantum computing:

The first phase is achieving "quantum computational supremacy," where a quantum computer outperforms classical supercomputers in solving specific prob-lems. This phase can be further divided into the quantum supremacy stage and the NISQ (Noisy Intermediate-Scale Quantum) stage. Achieving quantum suprem-acy requires coherent manipulation of approximately 50 qubits. The NISQ era, the second phase of quantum supremacy, will see the development of quantum computers with 50–100 qubits capable of tasks beyond the current capabilities of classical computers. Devices using NISQ technology will become useful tools for exploring many-body quantum physics. Google in the United States first achieved "quantum computational supremacy" in 2019 with its superconducting circuit system. China achieved this in the photonic quantum system in 2020 and the superconducting circuit system in 2021. Canada's Xanadu Company further broke through in the photonic quantum system's "quantum computational supremacy" in 2022.

The second phase involves realizing specialized quantum simulators capable of coherently manipulating hundreds of qubits and applying them to problems like combinatorial optimization, quantum chemistry, machine learning, etc., to guide material design, drug development, and more. Due to qubits' susceptibility to environmental noise, ensuring the correct operation of a scaled quantum bit system through quantum error correction is a necessity and a major challenge for some time.

The third phase is realizing programmable universal quantum computers, capable of coherently manipulating at least several million qubits, with significant applications in classical cryptography, large data searches, AI, etc. Due to technical difficulties, it's unclear when universal quantum computers will be realized, with the international academic community generally estimating at least 15 years or more.

4.4.2 How Far Is the Universal Quantum Computer?

The disruptive potential of quantum computing is foreseeable, but due to ongoing technological development, quantum computing still faces significant challenges in transitioning from academic research to commercial application. Thus, there's still a considerable distance before quantum computing can be effectively integrated into productive and daily life.

Currently, the commercialization of quantum computing remains in a stage of technical exploration. While significant breakthroughs have been made in both theory and experiment, including achievements by countries like the United States, Europe, and China, commercial applications are still in their infancy, or in a phase of exploratory use.

One major challenge in building a quantum computer is mastering and controlling superposition and entanglement: without superposition, qubits would behave like classical bits and not be in multiple states simultaneously. Without entanglement, even if qubits are in a superposition state, they cannot generate additional insights through interaction, rendering computation impossible, as each qubit's state would remain independent of others.

The key to creating commercial value with qubits is effectively managing superposition and entanglement. Quantum coherence, where qubits are entangled, and a change in one affects all others, is crucial for quantum computation. However, interactions of quantum coherent entities with their environment lead to rapid loss of quantum properties, known as "decoherence."

Typically, quantum algorithms aim to minimize the number of gates required to complete computational tasks before decoherence and other error sources are impacted. This often necessitates a hybrid computational approach, transferring as much computation as possible from the quantum computer to a classical computer. Scientists generally agree that a handy quantum computer would require between 1,000 and 100,000 qubits.

However, skeptics like renowned quantum physicist Mikhail Dyakonov point out that the massive continuous parameters describing a useful quantum computer's state could also be its Achilles' heel. For example, a machine with 1,000 qubits would have 2^{1000} parameters, about 10^{300}, a number greater than the subatomic particles in the universe. Controlling these parameters effectively is a significant challenge. If these parameters cannot be effectively controlled and maintained, the performance and reliability of a quantum computer might be compromised, potentially a fatal flaw.

The threshold theorem posits that infinite quantum computation is possible if each qubit's error in each quantum gate is below a certain threshold at the cost of significantly increasing the number of required qubits. Extra qubits are needed to form logical qubits from multiple physical qubits to handle errors, akin to error correction in current telecommunications, requiring additional bits to verify data. But this dramatically increases the number of physical qubits to be processed, already exceeding astronomical numbers.

For instance, a typical CMOS logic circuit used in classical computers has binary 0 represented by a voltage between 0 V and 1 V and binary 1 by 2 V and 3 V. Adding a 0.5 V noise to a binary 0 signal still yields the correct binary 0 recognition, demonstrating the robust noise resistance of classical computers that function correctly even with minor voltage fluctuations.

However, for a typical qubit, the energy difference between 0 and 1 is only 10^{-24} joules, a billionth of the energy of an X-ray photon. This tiny energy difference makes qubits highly sensitive to noise and interference, explaining why error correction is a huge challenge in quantum computing. Scientists worry that quantum error correction might incur significant overhead in auxiliary computation, complicating the development of quantum computers.

Furthermore, from a commercial perspective, nearly no companies in the quantum technology field have achieved cumulative profits. High technical barriers lead to billion-dollar R&D investments, while products remain in trial and error, making commercialization challenging. Doug Finke, who tracked over 200 quantum technology startups, predicts that most won't exist in ten years, at least not in their current form. He remarks, "There may be some winners, but many losers. Some will close, some will be acquired, some will merge." Additionally, there is no unified commercial quantum computing technology standard, as academia and industry develop various solid-state quantum system processors.

While quantum computing technology has achieved breakthroughs and continues to evolve, with significant investment from governments worldwide, there's still a journey ahead for true large-scale commercialization. Scaling up requires stable technology, fundamentally different from experimental or small-scale applications.

Quantum computing still grapples with challenges in the physical proof phase. While theoretically mature, entering the physical proof phase requires making the elusive and highly unstable quantum entanglement a manageable "stability" technology. Overall, the future of quantum computing is optimistic, and the journey toward commercialization of quantum computing is just beginning.

THE DISRUPTIVE FORCE OF
FUTURE COMPUTING

5.1 Solving the Computational Challenges of AI

With the explosion of technologies like ChatGPT, the advent of the AI "singularity" seems near. As a strategic technology leading this technological and Industrial Revolution wave, AI has become a new engine driving economic and social development. This has triggered a surge in computational power demands, challenging existing capacities. Without a significant enhancement in computational power, AI could hit a bottleneck. In this context, quantum computing emerges as a critical breakthrough in significantly boosting computational power.

5.1.1 The Rocky Start of AI

It was unexpected that AI and quantum computing would converge one day. AI, older than quantum computing, dates back to 1950 when Alan Turing proposed the famous "Turing Test" to determine computer intelligence. In 1956, the term "Artificial Intelligence" was coined at the Dartmouth Conference. Since then, AI has had a history of over seventy years.

However, AI's development has not been smooth sailing, often plunging into troughs after each surge. Achieving AI requires three elements: algorithms, data, and hardware computing power, each equally critical.

AI's early development focused on algorithms, or framework building, which is indispensable for AI. In 1961, the world's first industrial robot, Unimate, was trialed at a General Electric factory in New Jersey. In 1966, the mobile robot Shakey and the program Eliza emerged. Like the "grandmother" of today's Amazon Alexa, Google Assistant, and Apple's Siri, Eliza was a simple robotic program that engaged in pseudo-psychotherapy conversations via scripted responses.

Eliza's debut hinted at machines solving problems and interpreting spoken language. However, machines remained out of reach for abstract thinking, self-awareness, and natural language processing.

Despite these limitations, researchers remained optimistic about AI's future, predicting brilliant machines within twenty years. Unconditional support for AI research prevailed, epitomized by ARPA's then-director J.C.R. Licklider, who believed in funding people, not projects, allowing researchers to explore any interest.

However, AI's first winter soon arrived. By the early 1970s, criticism mounted as even the most advanced AI programs could only solve the simplest parts of the problems they were designed to tackle. Essentially, all AI programs were "toys," incapable of more complex tasks. Due to technological stagnation, investors began withdrawing from AI research.

For instance, the National Research Council in the US ceased its $20 million funding. In 1973, Lighthill's report critiqued British AI research for failing to achieve its "grandiose objectives," leading to a research lull in the UK. DARPA, disappointed with Carnegie Mellon University's speech understanding project, cut its annual funding of $3 million. By 1974, funding for AI projects had become scarce.

The reasons were multifaceted: the three elements necessary for AI were lacking then. AI programs could only address specific problems with limited complexity and objects. Moreover, computers, though seemingly massive, had minimal memory capacity, slow read / write speeds, and limited CPU capabilities, making them unsuitable for solving practical AI problems. Furthermore, AI required vast data for "intelligence" training, but the capacity to store and manage such data was severely limited.

This chapter of AI's history reflects its struggle to overcome technological and infrastructural barriers, marking a critical period in its evolution.

5.1.2 AI Approaches the "Singularity"

AI experienced a near-decade of dormancy after its first winter. The resurgence began with Harvard PhD Paul Werbos applied the concept of backpropagation (BP) in neural networks, proposing the Multilayer Perceptron (MLP), which includes input, hidden, and output layers, forming the basis of Artificial Neural Network (ANN). Subsequently, machine learning began to rise globally, encompassing not only neural networks but also Decision Tree Algorithms (ID3), Support Vector Machines (SVM), AdaBoost (ensemble learning), and more.

In 1989, LeCun combined backpropagation with weight-sharing convolutional layers to invent the Convolutional Neural Network (CNN), which was first successfully applied in handwritten character recognition systems for the US Postal Service. A typical CNN comprises input, convolutional, pooling, and fully connected layers. Convolutional layers extract local features from images, pooling layers significantly reduce the parameter scale (dimensionality reduction), and fully connected layers resemble traditional neural networks to output desired results.

AI's success and rapid Internet development accelerated innovative AI research, pushing the technology toward practical application. However, during this period, AI's intelligence lacked autonomy and strong reasoning ability, relying more on human programming for visual recognition functions.

Post-2016, with the advancement of big data, cloud computing, the Internet, the IoT, and ubiquitous sensory data, AI technologies, represented by deep neural networks, soared. They bridged the technical gap between science and application, achieving breakthroughs in image classification, speech recognition, Q&A, human-computer gaming, autonomous driving, and more, marking a new climax in AI development.

The 2022 launch of ChatGPT further propelled explosive growth in AI, ushering humanity into the AI era. Leveraging massive data sets, ChatGPT achieved enhanced language comprehension, becoming a versatile task assistant across various industries. ChatGPT opened doors to general AI applications.

However, ChatGPT's success also sparked a surge in computational power demands. According to OpenAI, ChatGPT's training involved 175 billion parameters and 45 TB of data, generating 4.5 billion words daily, requiring at least ten thousand Nvidia GPUA100s, with a single model training cost exceeding $12 million.

Although OpenAI didn't disclose GPT-4's exact parameter size, industry insiders speculate it's in the trillion range, necessitating even more powerful computational support.

This chapter highlights AI's journey toward the "singularity," facing computational challenges and driving the quest for enhanced capabilities. AI's trajectory, marked by milestones and challenges, illustrates its evolving nature and the growing need for advanced computing solutions.

5.1.3 AI Needs Quantum Computing

As one of the three pillars of AI, computational power constructs the underlying logic of AI. It supports algorithms and data, with the computational power level determining the data processing capability. Powerful computing is needed in the process of AI model training and inference. With the increasing intensity and complexity of computations, the requirement for computational precision is also rising.

In the 1970s, Intel integrated the CPU, which for a long time played the role of processing data, evolving by Moore's Law. Subsequently, Nvidia innovatively introduced the concept of the GPU. The key performance of a GPU lies in parallel computing, allowing complex problems to be divided into simpler ones and processed simultaneously, unlike the CPU, which processes sequentially.

Before 2008, GPUs were merely "accelerators" for image rendering. However, Nvidia's introduction of the CUDA architecture transformed GPUs into general-purpose processors. In 2012, Hinton and others miraculously improved the success rate of visual recognition from 74% to 85% using deep learning and GPUs, leading to the widespread application of GPUs in AI.

GPUs can provide performance tens or even hundreds of times better than CPUs. For instance, in 2011, Andrew Ng of Google Brain replaced 2,000 CPUs with 12 GPUs to enable a machine to recognize cats within a week through deep neural network learning. Although GPUs significantly outperform CPUs in computation speed, they share a common drawback of high power consumption. For example, the 2016 AlphaGo used over a thousand CPUs and over a hundred GPUs, costing $3,000 in electricity per game.

Consequently, scientists turned to FPGAs and ASICs. Compared to GPUs/CPUs, FPGAs/ASICs have a better performance-to-power consumption ratio, requiring significantly less power to achieve the same deep learning algorithm performance.

FPGAs (Field-Programmable Gate Arrays) allow users to design hardware circuits using Hardware Description Language based on their needs. They require much less memory bandwidth than GPUs or CPUs and are characterized by pipeline processing and rapid response. ASICs (Application-Specific Integrated

Circuits), such as Google's TPU, Qualcomm's Zeroth, IBM's TrueNorth, Nvidia's Tesla, Vimicro's NPU, and Cambrian's AI chips, are designed for specific purposes.

From CPUs and GPUs to FPGAs and ASICs, computational power has continuously improved, power consumption has reduced, and sizes have shrunk. However, an unavoidable fact is that all integrated circuits will eventually face the constraints of Moore's Law.

In 1965, Intel co-founder Gordon Moore predicted that the number of components on an integrated circuit would double every 18 to 24 months. Moore's Law summarizes the pace of progress in information technology and has profound global implications. However, classical computers, based on "silicon transistors," will eventually face physical limitations.

As transistors in computers get smaller, the barriers between them become thinner. At 3 nanometers, there are only about a dozen atoms of separation. In such a microscopic system, electrons can exhibit quantum tunneling, making it difficult to precisely represent "0" and "1," leading to the so-called "ceiling" of Moore's Law. Although researchers have proposed using different materials to strengthen transistor barriers, the fact remains that no material can prevent electron tunneling. In other words, under physical constraints, the improvement of computational power is ultimately limited.

Furthermore, increasing the number of data centers to address classical computational limitations is impractical due to sustainability and energy reduction requirements. According to the International Energy Agency, data centers account for 1.5% to 2% of global electricity consumption, roughly equivalent to the entire UK economy's usage. This proportion is expected to rise to 4% by 2030. AI is not only power-hungry but also water intensive. Google's 2023 environmental report revealed that in 2022, it consumed 5.6 billion gallons (approx. 21.2 billion liters) of water, equivalent to 37 golf courses. Over 5.2 billion gallons were used for data centers, a 20% increase from 2021.

Therefore, for AI to advance, finding a way to increase computational power while reducing energy consumption is crucial. In this context, AI must seek new computing methods, with quantum computing potentially being a significant breakthrough.

Current AI systems use hundreds or thousands of GPUs to enhance computational capabilities, significantly boosting learning or intelligence processing. However, these systems require large hardware cabinets and corresponding facilities, with larger AI hardware systems occupying almost half a football field.

As a key exploration direction for a leap in computational power, quantum computing holds the potential for far surpassing classical computing in parallel processing. Based on the superposition characteristic of quantum bits, quantum computing is akin to the "5G" of the computing realm, bringing not just speed but a fundamental change.

Once the number of qubits in a quantum chip reaches a certain level, the computing power will suffice for AI's computational demands. What previously required thousands of computers for AI might only need one quantum computer. The immense processing power of quantum computing could completely break the current computational limits of large AI models, propelling AI to another significant leap.

As quantum computing evolves, it will likely revolutionize AI, overcoming existing physical and energy constraints. Although quantum computing in AI is still in its nascent stages, it already promises a fascinating and powerful technological force.

5.2 When Quantum Computing Meets AI

Quantum computing is increasingly recognized as another powerful driver of progress in the digital society. Unlike some incremental technologies in the scientific community, quantum computing offers a disruptive enhancement in computational power, revolutionizing the traditionally dominant electronic computing, which relies on electrons as the primary carrier. Quantum computing, fundamentally, is a core element of digital technology and a driving force in the digital economy era.

Against this backdrop, the convergence of quantum computing and AI has garnered widespread attention. What future will this combination of disruptive technologies lead us to?

5.2.1 Quantum Computing Enhancing AI

From the perspective of quantum computing, quantum computers can process complex tasks at unprecedented speeds, redefining the concept of traditional computation.

For AI, machine learning models often face combinatorial optimization problems involving numerous variables and complex calculations. Even with advanced AI technologies, solving these problems on traditional computers remains time-consuming and challenging to find optimal solutions.

However, combining AI with quantum computers, based on quantum mechanics, could solve these problems instantaneously. Quantum computers can recognize data patterns that are elusive for traditional computers. In other words, advancements in quantum computing could further enhance the efficiency of machine learning, leading to higher-quality generalization abilities. This intersection of quantum computers and machine learning is known as QAI.

It's worth noting that quantum computing can't be directly used for machine learning, as classical algorithms on quantum computers don't achieve acceleration. Instead, specific QAI algorithms must be designed. Training data for QAI first need to be loaded in a format recognizable by quantum computers. After processing by QAI algorithms, the output is in a quantum format and requires measurement to read the final results.

Quantum algorithms originated in the late 20th century, with the most representative ones being Shor's algorithm for large number factorization and Grover's algorithm for accelerated searching. Quantum algorithms specifically for AI also emerged in the 1990s.

In 1995, Professor Kak from Louisiana State University first introduced the concept of quantum neural computing in "On Quantum Neural Computing." Researchers, including Professor Behrman, then proposed various quantum neural network models.

Currently, quantum machine learning algorithms largely follow the framework of traditional machine learning, replacing computationally intensive parts with quantum versions to improve overall efficiency.

Mainstream quantum machine learning algorithms include Quantum K-Means, Quantum Split Clustering, Quantum KNN, Quantum Support Vector Machine (QSVM), Quantum Decision Trees, Quantum Neural Networks (QNNs), Quantum Principal Component Analysis, Quantum Boltzmann Machines, Quantum Linear Discriminant Analysis, and more.

K-Means, a popular machine learning algorithm, uses proximity as a sample similarity index. In 2013, MIT's Lloyd and others proposed the Quantum K-Means algorithm, using the principle of superposition in linear space for parallel operations on multiple states, significantly outperforming classical computation.

In 2015, Pan Jianwei's team verified Quantum K-Means physically for 4, 6, and 8 qubit scales using a small-scale photonic quantum computer. Differentiating distances and inner products between high-dimensional vectors, common in traditional machine learning, can be efficiently performed on quantum computers.

Microsoft's Janyce Wiebe proposed the Quantum KNN algorithm following Lloyd's research approach. Using quantum algorithms to calculate distances between a test sample and all training features achieves polynomial acceleration. Selecting the smallest distances with Grover's amplitude estimation algorithm achieves quadratic acceleration.

In the SVM approach, QSVM has been experimentally validated on NMR platforms. In 2015, researchers built a 4-qubit QSVM, training it with standard font numbers 6 and 9 and then conducting binary classification tests on handwritten digits. Results confirmed the physical feasibility of QSVM.

5.2.2 Advantages of QAI

QAI is amassing a new kind of power, attracting even more attention than any other domain within quantum computing.

First, quantum machine learning can accelerate computation. One obvious way quantum can help is by speeding up classical techniques. The HHL algorithm allows for general acceleration in linear algebra but only applies to native quantum data and output. The Grover algorithm permits a general square acceleration in many unstructured search applications. However, the challenge for most attempts to directly accelerate traditional machine learning techniques is the need for efficient data loading, followed by superposition querying by the quantum device.

Second, quantum machine learning offers expanded computational space. Microsoft suggests that the field of quantum machine learning should set aside the "big data" problem and focus instead on "small data, big computation" problems. These problems seek to benefit from large computational workspaces, something unique that quantum computers can provide due to the immense Hilbert space of quantum bit systems.

Xanadu, a photonic quantum computing company based in Toronto, Canada, points out that many of the most promising QML (Quantum Machine Learning) techniques are best understood as akin to kernel methods in classical machine learning.

In traditional machine learning, kernel methods are a common technique that maps data from the original feature space to a higher-dimensional feature space to solve nonlinear problems that are difficult to handle in the original space. This mapping is achieved through kernel functions, including linear, polynomial, and Gaussian radial basis function kernels.

In the QML domain, some cutting-edge techniques are similar to kernel methods in traditional machine learning. This means that some QML methods can perform a feature mapping similar to traditional kernel methods in quantum space, allowing for higher-dimensional data processing and more complex nonlinear tasks. By drawing parallels with traditional kernel methods, scientists can better understand QML techniques and develop more efficient and innovative QML algorithms for broader applications and breakthroughs.

Additionally, IBM has published research on QNNs, showing that QNNs can handle higher-dimensional tasks compared to comparable classical neural networks and can deal with classically hard-to-simulate feature maps in terms of trainability. This indicates that quantum computing has advantages in certain cases and can be applied to more complex machine-learning tasks.

Pasqal, another company, released a bespoke framework using the reconfigurability of neutral atom devices to represent the kernel of graphs. This framework can process graph-structured problems, utilizing the properties of neutral atom devices in quantum computing for more efficient graph data processing.

Nonlinear systems of differential equations are a prominent set of problems that can be succinctly expressed but require many computational resources to solve numerically. These equations appear in various scientific and commercial applications where complex processes need to be modeled: from structural engineering to aerospace, from chemistry to biology, and from finance to epidemiology. For this, Qu&Co has developed a new technique for handling nonlinear differential equations on near-term quantum computers, namely differentiable quantum circuits. This method trains QNNs to use the large Hilbert space to handle derivatives. Qu&Co has also extended this approach to stochastic differential equations and has filed a patent application covering its technology.

Cambridge Quantum has identified QNLP as a special domain of QML. In 2021, they reported the first experimental results. Using a 5Q IBM device, they encoded a data set containing 130 sentences and 105 noun phrases. QNLP takes advantage of the expanded computational space offered by quantum computers. The startling similarities between the formalism proposed by Cambridge Quantum and the ZX calculus of quantum mechanics could prove to be a fruitful approach. Perhaps, as Bob Coecke, Chief Scientist at Cambridge Quantum Mechanics, says, "Language is quantum native."

Last, QML can offer unique quantum data. An increasingly important focus is that when a data set has quantum correlations or quantum interference effects that need to be addressed, QML should be able to surpass classical machine learning. Work in 2021 has begun to formalize and structure this, applicable both to learning tasks and to generative models.

California Institute of Technology published a study in 2021 delineating the capabilities of different machine learning models: one is traditionally driven but uses the outputs of quantum systems, like physical experiments, analog quantum simulators, or iterations of VQAs; the other maintains quantum coherence during the learning process. A key result is that classically driven ML can perform well, with predictive accuracy in "average cases" comparable to the capabilities of fully quantum learning. Fully quantum learning offers further exponential advantages in predictive accuracy for "worst-case" scenarios.

5.3 Quantum Applications: The Right Time

With tech giants and leading research institutions delving deeper into quantum computing, its potential impact on AI and other technologies is becoming increasingly apparent.

5.3.1 When Disruption Adds to Disruption

If leveraging quantum computing's high parallelism to optimize traditional machine learning further is considered the most significant application of quantum computing in AI, then its derivative applications in AI will further break new ground.

For instance, game theory is widely applied in AI, especially in distributed AI and multi-agent systems. When quantum extensions merge with game theory to form quantum game theory, it offers new tools for solving problems in AI development. Quantum game theory models decision-making processes in games and uses methods from quantum mechanics to study and describe these phenomena. DeepMind's AlphaGo, under Google, is based on quantum game theory. In its debut year, AlphaGo defeated world-class Go player Lee Sedol, and the following year bested Ke Jie, propelling AI to a new pinnacle.

Moreover, in semantic analysis of natural language, whether using AI or quantum computing, both share certain mathematical structural similarities. Quantum algorithms are exceptionally suitable for simulating quantum systems. Using quantum computing characteristics can more effectively address ambiguities in semantics, meaning that processing speed can be greatly enhanced in natural language processing with the help of quantum computing.

Additionally, pattern recognition, such as object recognition, is a crucial area in AI. However, AI researchers often only consider recognizing and distinguishing classical objects. With the growing development and attention to quantum computing, researchers have studied quantum measurement discrimination after addressing quantum gates. They found that rapid recognition can be achieved with minimal queries through optimal protocol design, demonstrating the discerning capability of quantum operations.

Conversely, AI can also help solve complex quantum problems. For instance, synthesizing drugs and processing different chemical reactions, which are difficult to simulate by solving quantum equations, can be addressed with AI methods. Similarly, AI techniques can also assist in solving the ground state energy problem of quantum many-body Hamiltonians.

Whether applying quantum technology to AI to further its development or using AI to address complex quantum issues, quantum computing, as a disruptive technology, urgently needs development, especially as Moore's Law approaches its physical limits.

5.3.2 Quantum AI in Practice: Venturing Deeper into Industries

The convergence of quantum computing and AI heralds a technological revolution in various sectors.

Finance and Banking

The financial sector is gradually feeling the impact of quantum AI. Quantum AI can enhance risk assessment, fraud detection, portfolio management, and option pricing, optimizing machine learning algorithms. High-frequency trading may be disrupted due to the speed of quantum computing.

Research has developed QNN models for predicting stock market behavior. Theoretically, QNNs offer a range of compelling advantages, including exponential storage capacity, simple structural design, enhanced stability, rapid computation, and resistance to catastrophic forgetting. Researchers have developed a stock market prediction model based on Quantum Elman Neural Network (QENN) and validated its performance. They used an innovative approach of adjusting the learning rate with a quantum version of the genetic algorithm. Then, they utilized quantum computing's parallel processing to access all possible states of QENN, further improving prediction accuracy.

Biomedicine

In biomedicine, quantum AI can accelerate drug discovery, improve medical imaging accuracy and speed, and optimize genetic analysis. Especially in drug development, scientists often need to simulate large molecules to understand their structure and function. Quantum computers can perform such simulations more accurately and efficiently, allowing scientists to predict molecular interactions better, thus accelerating drug design and optimization.

Turing Quantum has made significant breakthroughs in AI drug development, introducing a series of quantum AI application modules such as QuOmics, QuChem, QuDocking, and QuSynthesis, with ongoing development of QuProtein and QuDynamics. They have utilized tensor network technology to achieve a 38-fold acceleration in quantum AI drug design. As the number of simulated qubits increases, acceleration will improve, allowing quantum computing tools to solve practical problems even before the widespread application of general-purpose quantum computers.

Turing Quantum's quantum algorithms have significantly improved classic generative models for genomics and drug molecular structure design, enhancing algorithm convergence stability. During the pandemic, a team led by Jin Xianmin from Shanghai Jiao Tong University, in collaboration with a top-tier hospital, Nankai University, Imperial College London, and Carnegie Mellon University, used a quantum generative adversarial network model based on style mixing for predicting the variant structures of the coronavirus. The fidelity between the generated RNA structures and COVID-19 samples exceeded 95%, showing biological significance. The QNN maintained high consistency with classical algorithms thanks to quantum-inspired fuzzy convolution and progressive training modules. Discriminator models supported by quantum circuits also significantly stabilized GAN convergence. In scenarios of repurposing old drugs, the introduction of quantum algorithms notably enhanced the effectiveness of molecular structure generation, showing strong complementarity with classical algorithms.

The Future with Quantum AI

While the full potential of quantum computing is yet to be realized, its true impact on AI applications may take some time to emerge. However, it's certain that when quantum algorithms are fully integrated into the AI domain, they will solve some of the most frustrating and complex problems in business, administration, medicine, engineering, and more. The combined power of AI and quantum computing could lead to more efficient navigation systems, advanced automation technologies, precise drug development, accurate medical diagnostics, and effective supply chain management.

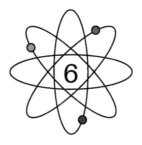

GOD DOES NOT PLAY DICE

6.1 The Century-Long Quantum Debate

The fifth Solvay Conference stands as one of the most famous gatherings in the history of quantum theory. This meeting, akin to a battle of the gods in physics, saw the world's leading physicists come together, forming an all-star lineup. Here, the epic debate between Einstein and Bohr over quantum mechanics began.

It was the persistent debates between these two masters that matured quantum mechanics, filling gaps in its theory. Einstein remained skeptical of quantum theory and Bohr's interpretation, proposing thought experiments to prove its incompleteness and absurdity. These debates continued in the physics community even after their deaths, but ironically, experimental results never seemed to favor Einstein. In quantum theory, the titan of physics appeared to have stumbled.

6.1.1 Einstein's Disbelief in Quantum Mechanics

Quantum mechanics, by principle, suggests that the world is a game of chance, much like gambling. It posits that all matter, made of atoms and subatomic particles, is governed by probability, not certainty, fundamentally suggesting that nature is built on randomness, a notion counterintuitive to human perception. Many found this hard to accept, including Einstein.

Einstein and Bohr, pioneers of quantum mechanics, had starkly opposing interpretations. Einstein struggled to believe that probabilities could dictate reality, famously declaring, "God does not play dice." His disbelief sparked a century-long debate over quantum mechanics.

His famous quote can summarize Einstein's perspective. He emphasized that quantum mechanics could not have action at a distance, upholding classical theory's "locality" principle.

Einstein argued that the three basic assumptions of classical physics—conservation laws, determinism, and locality—should be common to both classical and quantum mechanics. The conservation laws include energy, momentum, angular momentum, etc. Determinism in classical physics leads to definite solutions, like predicting an object's exact position using Newtonian mechanics.

Locality, or causality, means an object can only be affected by its immediate surroundings, implying that interactions between two objects must be mediated by waves or particles. As per relativity, information cannot travel faster than light, so an event at one point cannot instantaneously affect another. This led Einstein to describe instant interactions between particles as "spooky action at a distance." Notably, classical physics before quantum theory were also local theories.

In contrast, Bohr believed measurement changes everything. He argued that particles remain indeterminate until observed. For instance, in the double-slit experiment, electrons can appear almost anywhere within a probabilistic range until detected, with their location indeterminacy disappearing at the moment of observation.

Bohr's principle of quantum mechanics states that measuring a particle forces it to abandon its potential states, choosing a definite position where it's found. He contended that the nature of reality is inherently vague and uncertain, a notion Einstein couldn't accept. Einstein believed in the certainty of things, that they exist independently of observation, famously stating, "I like to think the moon is there even if I am not looking at it." He thus believed quantum theory was incomplete, lacking details on particle characteristics, like their positions when unobserved. However, his views were nearly solitary in the physics community then.

At the fifth Solvay Conference, Einstein and Bohr had their first round of debate, focusing on Heisenberg's Uncertainty Principle. According to this principle, momentum and position information cannot be known simultaneously; knowing one inevitably alters the other, embodying the quantum world's inherent uncertainty. Einstein presented an upgraded single-slit experiment to challenge this.

In this modified experiment, a spring was attached to the slit barrier, allowing vertical movement. As an electron passes through the slit, it would affect the spring's momentum, causing vertical movement. Since the electron's position is already determined while passing through the slit, observing the spring's movement should, in theory, reveal the electron's momentum, seemingly knowing both its position and momentum simultaneously.

After discussing with fellow physicists, Bohr concluded that if the spring is sensitive enough to react to an electron, the entire apparatus operates at the quantum level. Since the experiment is conducted in the quantum realm, the spring has inherent uncertainty, making it impossible to deduce the electron's momentum from observing the spring.

Einstein's thought experiment was effectively refuted by Bohr, marking Bohr's initial victory in this intellectual duel. This was just the beginning of their prolonged debate.

6.1.2 The "Photon Box" Challenge

Unsatisfied with his slight defeat in the first round, Einstein, after years of deep contemplation, re-challenged Bohr at the sixth Solvay Conference in 1930.

In the autumn of 1930, the sixth Solvay Conference convened in Brussels. Well-prepared, Einstein presented his famous thought experiment—the "Photon Box," targeting another pair of uncertainties in Heisenberg's principle—time and energy. Heisenberg's principle suggests that reducing uncertainty in time would increase uncertainty in energy, as fundamental particles in the quantum world have fluctuating energy levels. According to Einstein's special relativity, energy and mass are interchangeable, meaning the mass of fundamental particles is always changing.

Einstein imagined a box with a small hole covered by a shutter controlled by a mechanical clock. The box contained a certain amount of radioactive material. The clock would open the hole at a specific moment, releasing a photon. The escape time of the photon could be precisely measured. Meanwhile, the box, hanging on a spring scale, would show a decrease in mass equivalent to the photon's mass, which, using the mass-energy equivalence $E = mc^2$, would indicate the energy loss. According to Einstein, this setup measured both time and energy precisely, disproving the uncertainty principle and challenging Bohr's viewpoint.

Einstein's Photon Box experiment initially took Bohr aback. However, miraculously, overnight, Bohr found a flaw in Einstein's experiment using Einstein's own theory of general relativity. Bohr pointed out that when the photon escaped, the box's reduced mass would cause it to rise. According to general relativity, any clock displacement along the gravitational field would alter its rate. Thus, the time read by the clock inside the box would change due to the photon's escape. In other words, if the photon's energy was to be measured, the moment of its escape could not be precisely controlled. Bohr deduced the uncertainty relation between energy and time using the redshift formula from general relativity.

Einstein was stunned by this counterargument. Although still unconvinced, he conceded that Bohr's interpretation of quantum mechanics had no logical flaws.

6.2   Einstein's Entanglement

The third round of the debate between Einstein and Bohr over quantum theory peaked in 1935. During this year, the concept of quantum entanglement, a crucial aspect of modern quantum mechanics, was born.

6.2.1 Inexplicable Phenomenon, Defying Space and Time

Amid Einstein and Bohr's debate, Einstein aimed to demonstrate the absurdity of quantum mechanics. In 1935, Einstein and colleagues Podolsky and Rosen published a paper titled "Can Quantum-Mechanical Description of Physical Reality Be Considered Complete?" This became known as the EPR paper, an acronym for their last names. The arguments presented in this paper are also known as the EPR paradox or Einstein's theory of local reality. In this paper, Einstein introduced a powerful concept named "quantum entanglement" by Schrödinger.

Einstein proposed a thought experiment describing a large unstable particle decaying into two smaller particles (A and B): a large particle splits into two identical smaller particles. These smaller particles, gaining kinetic energy, fly off in opposite directions. If particle A has an upward spin, particle B must have a downward spin to maintain overall spin conservation, and vice versa.

According to quantum mechanics, the two particles should be in a superposition state before measurement, like a 50%-50% probability mix of "A up, B down" and "A down, B up." Upon measuring A, its state collapses instantaneously. If A's state collapses to up, then B's state must be down due to conservation.

However, if particles A and B are light-years apart, quantum mechanics suggests that B should also have a 50%-50% probability of being up or down. How, then, does it always choose down the moment A collapses? Is there some way for A and B to "communicate" instantly? Assuming they could sense each other, their signaling would need to traverse light-years instantaneously, exceeding the speed of light, which contradicts existing physical knowledge. Thus, Einstein considered this a paradox.

Schrödinger, after reading the EPR paper, wrote a letter to Einstein in German, where he first used the term "Verschränkung" (meaning entanglement) to describe the enduring correlation between two temporarily coupled particles that persists even after they decouple, as seen in the EPR thought experiment.

Bohr responded to the EPR paradox. He believed that since the two particles formed an entangled whole, represented by a single wave function, measuring A's momentum already disrupted B's position information. Measuring B afterward means the information is no longer the same as before measuring A. The same applies vice versa; touching B would change A. The two particles are thus entangled, making simultaneous acquisition of a particle's position and momentum impossible. Bohr's view was that since A and B are correlated parts of a whole, they need not transmit any information to each other.

Nevertheless, Einstein never accepted Bohr's peculiar explanation. The divergence in their viewpoints persisted until their deaths, with no conclusive resolution.

6.2.2 Bell's Inequality

Committed to proving Einstein's hidden variable theory, which posited that the randomness of quantum entanglement was only superficial, physicist John Bell proposed an experiment to validate Einstein's stance.

According to deterministic birth theory, the polarization direction of photons is predetermined, making the measurement result of one photon unrelated to the other. However, quantum mechanics dictates that measuring one photon inevitably affects the result of the other's measurement.

For instance, consider four experimental setups with polarizers at angles (0°, 0°), (30°, 0°), (0°, −30°), and (30°, −30°). In the first setup, all photons would pass through the polarizers. The second and third scenarios involve adjusting each polarizer independently. In the fourth setup, both polarizers are rotated. Simply put, if the measurement results of one photon are unrelated to the other, the result with both polarizers rotated should be ≤ the sum of the results with each polarizer rotated separately. This forms the basis of Bell's inequality. Quantum theory suggests that the result with both polarizers rotated might exceed this sum.

Thus, if Bell's inequality holds, Einstein wins; if not, Bohr prevails. The inequality transformed the EPR paradox from a theoretical thought experiment into a feasible physical experiment. Despite Bell's intention to support Einstein by identifying hidden variables in quantum systems, the experimental outcomes didn't bolster Einstein's theory.

Finally, in 1946, physicist John Wheeler proposed the first experiment to achieve an entangled state using photons. Light, being a wave, has a vibration direction similar to how water waves move forward while each specific point on the water's surface vibrates up and down. Natural light, composed of randomly mixed light rays of various vibration directions, becomes "polarized light" when it passes through a polarizer, restricting it from vibrating only in a specific direction. Polarized sunglasses, for example, use a polarizer.

In laboratories, scientists use polarizers to measure and transform the polarization direction of light. Light can have different linear polarization directions, and perpendicular polarization directions can be analogized to electrons' up and down spins. Hence, a slight modification of the entangled state described using spins also applies to photons.

If the vibration direction of polarized light aligns with the axis of the polarizer, the light passes through; if perpendicular, it doesn't. If at a 45° angle, half the light passes, and half doesn't. However, quantum theory posits that light exhibits wave-particle duality, and in the lab, it's possible to emit individual photons by reducing light intensity.

Individual photons also carry polarization information. When a photon enters a polarizer, it only has two outcomes: pass or not. Therefore, when the polarization direction of an incident photon is at a 45° angle to the direction of the polarizer, each photon has a 50% probability of passing and 50% of not passing. If this angle is something other than 45°, the probability of passing is also a different number related to the angle.

This means photons can achieve entanglement and carry easily measurable properties like polarization, allowing scientists to design experiments to test Einstein's EPR paradox.

Utilizing this property of photons, John Wheeler pointed out that a pair of photons generated by the annihilation of an electron-positron pair should have two different polarization directions. Soon after, in 1950, Wu Jianxiong and Shakharov announced they had successfully realized this experiment, confirmed Wheeler's idea, and generated the first pair of entangled photons with opposite polarization directions in history.

6.2.3 Validating Quantum Entanglement

Quantum entanglement, akin to the mysterious phenomenon of "telepathy" where two distant strangers simultaneously think of doing the same thing as if an invisible thread connects them, is a similar marvel in the microscopic world. Two microscopic particles from a common source share an entangled relationship in quantum entanglement. These entangled particles, like telepathically connected twins, instantly mirror each other's state changes, no matter the distance between them—be it kilometers or further.

On October 4, 2022, at 17:45 Beijing time, the Nobel Prize in Physics was announced. It was awarded to French physicist Alain Aspect, American physicist John Clauser, and Austrian physicist Anton Zeilinger for "conducting experiments with entangled photons, refuting Bell's inequality, and pioneering quantum information science." This Nobel Prize acknowledges their foundational research in quantum information science and endorses the theories of quantum mechanics and entanglement.

Professor Clauser, one of the laureates, developed and conducted a practical quantum entanglement experiment based on John Bell's concept. John Clauser constructed a device that emitted two entangled photons toward polarizing filters. In 1972, together with his doctoral student Stuart Freedman, he demonstrated a result that violated Bell's inequality and aligned with the predictions of quantum mechanics. The fundamental aim of testing Bell's inequality was to ascertain the existence of hidden variables in quantum systems, verifying whether quantum mechanics is local or non-local.

However, Clauser's experiment had limitations—one being the low efficiency in preparing and capturing particles. Additionally, the experiment had loopholes since the measurements were preset, with fixed angles for the polarizing filters. Subsequently, Professor Aspect refined the experiment by changing the measurement settings after the entangled particles left the source, ensuring that the settings present at emission didn't influence the experiment's outcome.

Furthermore, through precise tools and experiments, Professor Zeilinger began utilizing entangled state quanta. His research team also demonstrated a phenomenon known as "quantum teleportation" (QT), enabling quantum movement from one particle to another over certain distances.

Over 50 years have passed since the introduction of Bell's inequality, Clauser's initial experiment, and subsequent experiments addressing loopholes. All these Bell test experiments have supported quantum theory, indicating the failure of local realism. The longstanding work of these three physicists on quantum mechanics ultimately validated quantum entanglement, an achievement of immense significance for modern technology. Thus, the century-long debate between Einstein and Bohr finally concluded.

6.3   Quantum Entanglement as a Powerful Tool

Quantum entanglement, a phenomenon where the state of one particle instantaneously influences another, irrespective of the distance separating them, is akin to a sort of "teleportation" in science fiction. However, it's not physical objects but merely the state of microscopic particles that instantaneously shifts, and only certain special states at that. This marvel has become the theoretical foundation of many scientific fantasies, particularly in quantum communication.

6.3.1 What Is Quantum Communication?

As a crucial part of the quantum revolution, "quantum communication" refers to a novel method of transmitting information using the effects of quantum entanglement.

To understand quantum entanglement, it's essential to note it's an incredibly peculiar and profound phenomenon in quantum mechanics. It describes a mysterious connection between two or more quantum particles whose states are interdependent and cannot be independently described. This implies that observing one particle's state instantly affects its entangled counterpart, regardless of their distance. Quantum entanglement, unlike anything in classical mechanics, operates exclusively within quantum systems.

For example, consider a basic particle with zero spins decaying into two particles spinning in opposite directions. When we measure one particle and find its spin up, the other must be down, and vice versa, to conserve overall spin.

Theoretically, quantum entanglement can occur over any distance, even across the universe. Measuring one particle instantly reveals the state of the other. This instant connection defies conventional physics and isn't limited by the speed of light.

Professor Pan Jianwei once experimented in Qinghai to measure the speed of particle entanglement. The results showed the minimum speed of quantum entanglement is 10,000 times the speed of light. This doesn't mean the speed of entanglement is exactly 10,000 times faster than light, but due to experimental constraints, this is the magnitude achieved.

However, quantum communication doesn't directly transmit information through entanglement. Instead, it uses quantum bits' unclonable and measurement-collapse properties for theoretically secure encryption.

In classical terms, it's easy to replicate a bit's state (0 or 1). If we have a bit in state 0, creating another bit in the same state is straightforward. Information is transmitted and processed in a replicable manner. Quantum mechanics, however, operates differently. The no-cloning theorem states that attempting to replicate an unknown quantum state inevitably alters the original state, leading to "measurement collapse."

The unclonability of quanta means attackers can't replicate transmitted quantum bits without detection. Even if they intercept these quanta, they can't copy them for further surveillance or analysis. Moreover, the phenomenon of quantum measurement collapse ensures that any attempt to measure or interfere with quantum bits during transmission causes the entangled state to collapse. By mixing some entangled particles with electromagnetic wave information, any eavesdropping attempt by spies triggers this collapse, which is simultaneously detected by the sender, alerting both sender and receiver and halting transmission on that channel. Additionally, the collapse triggered by the spy's attempt leaves them with information that does not represent the actual transmitted state.

6.3.2 Why Do We Need Quantum Communication?

The development of human society is inextricably linked to communication, essentially the transfer of information. In ancient times, when technology was limited, information transfer relied primarily on human carriers.

The evolution of information technology ushered us into the era of information communication. Significant milestones include Samuel Morse's first telegraph in 1844, Alexander Graham Bell's invention of the telephone in 1876, Heinrich Hertz's discovery of electromagnetic waves and validation of Maxwell's equations in 1887, and Guglielmo Marconi's patent for wireless telegraphy in 1895. These technological innovations revolutionized human communication. The advent of computers triggered even more advanced communication methods, leading us into the digital communication era that continues today.

However, most communication methods focus on more than just the reliable transmission of information, not its security, which relies on cryptography. Cryptographic systems are always at risk of being deciphered, especially with the advent of quantum computing, which can easily break many current cryptographic methods due to its parallel computing capabilities.

In traditional cryptography, the text to be secretly transmitted is called plaintext, and the transformed text is called ciphertext. Converting plaintext into ciphertext is encryption, and the reverse process is decryption. The rules used for encryption and decryption are known as keys. In modern communication, keys are generally specific computer algorithms.

Early cryptography used symmetric encryption, where the sender and receiver share a single key for encryption and decryption. Although this method is simple and technologically mature, it has a significant issue: secure key transmission.

The key must be sent to the receiver via another secure channel to ensure secure communication. If intercepted, the content of the communication is exposed. This issue led cryptographers to seek more secure solutions, giving rise to asymmetric encryption.

In asymmetric encryption, each individual in the communication process has a pair of keys: public and private. The public key encrypts information, while the private key decrypts it. The encryption algorithm is public, but the decryption algorithm is secret. As encryption and decryption are asymmetric, this technology is known as asymmetric encryption.

Importantly, it's challenging to derive the private key from the public key, meaning encryption is easy, but decryption is difficult. The most commonly used asymmetric encryption algorithm is RSA, which was developed by Ron Rivest, Adi Shamir, and Leonard Adleman.

RSA is based on a simple yet significant number theory fact: multiplying two primes is easy, but factoring their product is very hard. For instance, calculating $17 \times 37 = 629$ is straightforward, but finding the factors of 629 is much more difficult, especially with larger numbers.

For classical computers, cracking high-digit RSA encryption is nearly impossible. A machine capable of $1{,}0^{12}$ operations per second would take 150,000 years to break a 300-bit RSA encryption. However, for quantum computers, this is trivial. A quantum computer using Shor's algorithm can easily crack a 300-bit RSA encryption in less than a second.

Modern cryptographic analysis and hardware development, particularly quantum computing, pose a severe threat to information security. This is especially critical in military domains, where geopolitical conflicts are intensifying, and political, economic, military, and technological power struggles are escalating. Traditional territorial sovereignty in land, sea, and air faces increasing pressure from emerging domains like nuclear, space, and cyberspace. Future battlefields may span vast areas like the deep sea, outer space, and polar regions, encompassing physical, informational, cognitive, and social dimensions. To effectively organize and control these multidimensional battlefields, comprehensive and accurate intelligence, massive heterogeneous data, timely command information, and secure channels and platforms for information acquisition, transmission, and processing are essential.

With information and energy as strategic national resources, the development of quantum communication is becoming inevitable. The allure of quantum communication lies in its potential to transcend the limits of existing classical information systems and significantly enhance information security. This offers a significant sense of safety in a world lacking information security.

6.3.3 Will Quantum Communication Replace Traditional Communication?

As a technology promising absolute security, will quantum communication replace traditional communication? Despite its revolutionary potential, Quantum communication is intended to supplement traditional communication. Quantum and traditional communications complement each other, catering to different communication needs. Fundamentally, quantum communication is a different form of communication aimed at making traditional digital communication more secure.

First, regarding reliance on communication channels, quantum communication depends on traditional communication channels. Quantum information must be transmitted via fiber optics, microwave channels, or satellites, which are all part of traditional communication infrastructure. For instance, optical fibers, the main transmission medium in traditional communication, transmit electrical signals and Internet data. In quantum communication, photons serve as quantum bits for transmitting quantum information. Hence, optical fibers are also a core medium for quantum communication. Similarly, microwave channels commonly used in satellite communication can transmit microwave quantum states in quantum communication. Thus, traditional and quantum communications must collaborate to achieve secure end-to-end communication. However, for quantum communication, traditional classic communication technology transmission mediums need targeted optimization and upgrades to adapt to quantum communication use.

From the perspective of communication range, traditional communication technologies, including the Internet, mobile communication, cable television, and satellite communication, have established vast and complex global communication infrastructures. These technologies provide extensive coverage, including urban, rural, and remote areas. Internet connectivity is widespread globally, while mobile networks cover most densely populated regions. This broad coverage enables easy voice calls, data transfer, video conferencing, social media usage, and other communication activities, fulfilling daily life and business needs.

In contrast, quantum communication often has limited range due to factors like noise, light loss, and fiber-optic transmission limitations affecting quantum states. This restricts the wide application of quantum communication in global networks.

Furthermore, establishing a quantum communication network requires highly complex equipment and technology, making it costly. Being mature and less expensive, traditional communication technology is easier to implement.

As seen, quantum and traditional communications are complementary, each with its own advantages and applicable areas. Quantum communication can be viewed as a new battlefield and development opportunity alongside classical communication. Its security makes it promising in susceptible areas like government, military, and finance. However, traditional communication technology will continue to play a key role in global infrastructure, meeting various communication needs.

Therefore, quantum communication is not meant to replace but to cooperate with traditional communication, jointly building a more secure and robust network. These two forms of communication will collectively drive the development of the communication field in the future.

6.4 QKD: Making Information Impenetrable to Eavesdropping

Quantum communication utilizes physical entities like photons, atoms, molecules, and ions as carriers of information encoded in quantum states. It transmits these states through quantum channels to convey information. Currently, the two most typical applications of quantum communication are QKD and QT. QKD, in particular, is used for the secure transmission of classical information, ensuring that information is no longer susceptible to eavesdropping.

6.4.1 Key Distribution under Quantum Principles

To ensure information security, people encrypt information using keys before transmitting it to the recipient, who then decrypt it using the same key. The security of information thus relies on the security of the key.

In 1949, Claude Shannon, the founder of information theory, published the paper "Theory of Secrecy Systems," demonstrating that encrypted information is unbreakable if the key is as long as the plaintext and is used only once, commonly known as one-time pad encryption. However, risks still exist in the process of key distribution.

QKD applies fundamental quantum mechanics properties, ensuring that any attempt to intercept keys during transmission is detectable by legitimate users. Eavesdroppers attempting to intercept quantum keys must perform measurements, and according to quantum theory's uncertainty principle and measurement collapse, any measurement on quantum keys will inevitably affect the quantum system, altering its state. As a result, what the eavesdropper intercepts is no longer the original information, and both parties in communication can instantly detect the eavesdropper's presence and immediately cease communication. As the most secure method of key transmission, QKD achieves theoretical absolute information security.

QKD has two forms: Discrete Variable QKD (DV-QKD) and Continuous Variable QKD (CV-QKD). DV-QKD is based on discrete quantum states for transmitting information, typically using single-photon or polarized photon states. Well-defined basic units describe these quantum states, such as horizontal and vertical polarization.

In 1999, Australian scientist Ralph first proposed the concept of CV-QKD. CV-QKD uses continuous quantum states for transmitting information, typically the canonical components of the light field, like amplitude and phase. These continuous states can contain infinitely more information, making them more flexible than discrete states. This characteristic also gives CV-QKD unique performance advantages.

The setup for a CV-QKD system is relatively simple, requiring only a standard coherent laser and balanced homodyne detectors. Compared to DV-QKD, CV-QKD has more simplified hardware requirements, reducing system manufacturing costs and making it easier to implement and popularize. This feature is significant for practical applications, especially large-scale deployment and commercialization.

Under similar conditions, CV-QKD also exhibits a higher key distribution rate. The key distribution rate is an important metric for evaluating the performance of QKD systems. The output key rate of CV-QKD far exceeds DV-QKD technology, meaning it can generate keys more quickly, making it more suitable for high-speed data transmission and real-time communication applications. This efficiency is due to CV-QKD's utilization of the continuous nature of the light field, allowing each quantum bit to carry more information.

Additionally, CV-QKD is highly compatible with traditional optical communication networks. The relatively simple hardware required for CV-QKD systems can seamlessly integrate with existing fiber-optic communication infrastructure. This offers greater convenience and scalability for practical applications, while DV-QKD systems might need more modifications and investment to be compatible with traditional networks.

6.4.2 Creating Unbreakable Quantum Communication

The world's first QKD protocol, BB84, was introduced in 1984 by American physicist Charles H. Bennett and Canadian cryptographer Gilles Brassard. Named after the initials of their surnames and the year of its inception, the BB84 protocol is based on quantum mechanics principles. It leverages the properties of quantum states to create unbreakable keys.

To understand the BB84 protocol, we must first consider its communicators, Alice and Bob. Alice is the sender, while Bob is the receiver. Their goal is to establish a shared, secure key without eavesdropping.

Alice uses quantum states, specifically the polarization states of single photons, for this purpose. These photons can be polarized differently, and Alice opts for two sets of non-orthogonal basis vectors, each comprising two orthogonal polarization states.

The chosen basis vectors are rectilinear basis vectors: Horizontal (H) and Vertical (V) polarization states; diagonal basis vectors: +45-degree and −45-degree polarization states.

Alice encodes classical bit information (0s and 1s) onto these quantum states. She assigns H and −45-degree polarization to represent 0, while V and +45-degree polarization represent 1.

Once encoded, Alice sends these photons to Bob, who randomly selects a set of basis vectors to measure the photons and record the outcomes. This step is crucial as Bob's measurements inevitably alter the states of the photons. Later, Alice and Bob publicly announce their chosen basis vectors over a public channel. This step is open but does not reveal the actual content of the information.

Next, Alice and Bob each retain the information aligned with the previously announced basis vectors. These are known as "sifted keys" and are known only to them. They then sample a portion of their sifted keys to check for consistency.

If the error rate in this comparison exceeds a certain threshold, they consider the communication insecure and discard the key. They can then continue with another round until they acquire a sifted key with an acceptable error rate.

Finally, once the security of the sifted key is assured, Alice and Bob can perform further data processing, including error correction and privacy amplification, to generate a final secure key. This key can be used to encrypt and decrypt their communication.

Today, nearly forty years after its development, various QKD protocols based on different quantum mechanics properties have been proposed. While some typical QKD protocols have been rigorously proven secure, practical QKD systems still face security vulnerabilities due to imperfect devices. Fortunately, after over three decades of global academic collaboration, a combination of "Measurement-Device-Independent QKD" protocols and precisely calibrated, autonomously controlled quantum communication systems can now provide security under real-world conditions.

6.4.3 QKD Moves toward Practical Application

The practical application research of QKD is progressing rapidly.

In 2021, a team led by Pan Jianwei at the University of Science and Technology of China demonstrated an integrated space-to-ground quantum communication network. Based on the Micius quantum satellite, integrating fiber and free-space QKD links, this network allows any user within it to communicate with any other user over a total distance of up to 4,600 km. In the same year, a team led by Feng Zhao at the university showcased a 10 m underwater channel-based polarization-encoded QKD experiment with a secure key generation rate exceeding 700 kpbs. In 2022, Guo Guangcan's team at the same university achieved 833 km fiber QKD, extending the world record for unrelay-assisted QKD secure transmission distance by over 200 km, marking a significant step toward realizing 1,000 km land-based quantum-secured communication.

Regarding applications, QKD-related products have formed a complete product system from terminal devices, network devices, and application devices to application software.

With the commercialization of high-speed polarization-encoded QKD devices, key exchange cryptosystems, and quantum-secure encryption routers, companies like QuantumCTek are offering comprehensive, commercially compliant solutions, covering most application scenarios including urban, intercity, and special channels, taking a leading position globally. Based on this, China has built the world's first thousand-kilometer-level quantum-secured communication "Beijing–Shanghai Trunk Line," the largest quantum metropolitan network in terms of scale and coverage in Hefei, and the first phase of the national wide-area quantum-secured communication backbone network. The Chinese quantum-secured communication backbone network now covers key national strategic regions like Beijing-Tianjin-Hebei, the Yangtze River Delta, and the Greater Bay Area, extending over 10,000 km and including ground stations in Beijing, Chongqing, Guangzhou, and other cities to interface with satellites like Micius.

QKD provides key and data security coordination, monitoring, and resistance to quantum computing-based cyber-attacks for government application systems in the government sector. For instance, South Korea is constructing a 2,000 km QKD network covering 48 government departments. The aforementioned "Hefei Quantum Metropolitan Network" is based on constructing the e-government external network, providing quantum security access services to nearly 500 party and government agencies at the municipal and district levels. Additionally, cities like Jinan and Haikou are exploring related applications.

In the financial sector, QKD offers secure transmission guarantees for internal network or data center information transmission and sensitive communication in financial systems. For example, the American company Quantum Xchange utilizes QKD to provide secure information transmission for multiple users between Wall Street's financial market and New Jersey's operational backend. In China, since 2012, companies like QuantumCTek have been expanding related applications under the guidance of the People's Bank of China (Central Bank) and the China Banking and Insurance Regulatory Commission. The Central Bank conducted a quantum application demonstration project for the cross-border RMB payment information management system, with major banks like ICBC, Agricultural Bank of China, Bank of China, and Construction Bank participating in the pilot.

In the power sector, QKD can enhance the security capabilities of power dispatch automation, distribution automation, and electricity information collection. The Oak Ridge National Laboratory, Los Alamos National Laboratory, and EPB Communications Technology Company in the US have collaborated to research and validate the efficacy of QKD systems in safeguarding the national power grid. In China, the State Grid has undertaken a series of business explorations in different optical cable types, quantum networks, and power grid services in Beijing, Shanghai, Anhui, Jiangsu, Zhejiang, Shandong, Xinjiang, and other regions. In addition to these sectors, telecommunication, industrial Internet, autonomous driving, and healthcare are also exploring the practical applications of QKD technology.

6.4.4 Technical Challenges of Quantum Key Distribution

Despite significant research achievements in QKD, two major challenges currently remain: achieving higher key generation rates (encoding rates) and extending the key transmission distance.

On the one hand, the current theoretical and experimental work on QKD has not yet broken through the limits of the key generation rate distance in un relay scenarios. This means that our current methods for transmitting quantum keys have not surpassed traditional classical physical constraints. Distance becomes a limiting factor without relays due to the attenuation of quantum states during transmission. As the distance increases, the number of photons decreases, reducing the number of photons received by the receiving device per unit time and thus affecting the key distribution rate. This problem can be partially alleviated by increasing photon emission rates and using more efficient detectors, but challenges persist in long-distance transmissions.

Another limiting factor is the noise in measuring devices. Even under ideal conditions, measuring devices introduce a certain level of noise. With increasing distance, signal attenuation leads to fewer photons received by the measuring device, increasing the relative proportion of noise. When the noise ratio exceeds a certain threshold, key distribution becomes unfeasible. This limits the performance of QKD systems in long-distance communication because as the signal strength reduces, noise relatively increases, thus limiting the available key generation rate.

Scientists are actively researching improvements and innovations in QKD technology to address these issues. Some approaches include using quantum repeaters to enhance signal strength, reduce attenuation, and improve the performance of measuring devices to lower noise levels. Additionally, new QKD protocols and techniques, such as continuous variable QKD, are being proposed to increase the flexibility and performance of QKD systems.

While QKD, as a quantum mechanics-based encryption communication technology, has tremendous theoretical potential, it still faces practical limitations in encoding rate and distance. Continuous research and technological innovation are underway to overcome these limitations and enhance the performance of QKD systems, enabling more secure long-distance communications. It is foreseeable that with the ongoing development of quantum technology, QKD is expected to become a key security technology with broader applications in the future.

6.5 QT: Instantaneous Information Transmission

Beyond Quantum Key Distribution, QT serves as another typical application of quantum communication. It is an effective means of transferring quantum information and is expected to become a primary method of information exchange in applications such as distributed quantum computing networks.

6.5.1 What Is QT?

While QKD utilizes quantum channels to transmit classical information, QT transfers quantum bits (qubits) from one party to another via quantum channels, directly enabling the transmission of information. QT is also known as quantum remote transmission or QT.

QT resembles the concept of teleportation in science fiction movies, but instead of moving objects, it instantly transfers information, not physical matter. Leveraging quantum entanglement effects, QT can seemingly make a quantum state disappear in one place and instantaneously appear in another. The "instantaneously" here refers to a physical instant, not requiring any time.

The basic principle of QT involves two parties, Alice and Bob, with a potential eavesdropper, Eve. The process begins with the creation of an entangled state. One common method of creating an entangled state is through a process where interaction between two bits entwines their states, rendering them inseparable. For example, consider a system containing two qubits, A and B. Initially, A and B can be in any quantum state, but when they interact to enter a special state, they form an entangled pair. This process is mathematically described, showing a special relationship between the states of A and B. A common entangled state is the Bell state, a particular two-bit state establishing entanglement between A and B. If Alice controls A, B is with Bob in this entangled pair.

Next is Alice's measurement process, a critical step in QT. Assuming Alice wishes to transmit a qubit, the "bit to be transmitted" is denoted as C. She needs to perform a joint measurement on the bit to be sent (C) and her part of the entangled state (A), known as a Bell measurement. Bell measurement is a method for measuring the entanglement between two quantum bits, with four possible outcomes.

Outcome 1: If Alice's measurement result is 1, she must convey this result to Bob.

Outcome 2: If Alice's measurement result is 2, she must give it to Bob.

Outcome 3: If Alice's measurement result is 3, she must convey this result to Bob.

Outcome 0: If Alice's measurement result is 0, she must get this result to Bob.

Once Alice completes the measurement and conveys the impact to Bob, Bob performs a series of operations on his part of the entangled state (B) based on the received result to restore the state of the bit to be transmitted (C). This operation process depends on the Bell measurement outcome, instructing Bob on how to manipulate his entangled state.

If Alice's measurement result is 1, Bob must perform a series of operations on his entangled state to transform it into the state of the bit to be transmitted (C). If Alice's measurement result is 2, 3, or 0, Bob must take different actions to evolve the entangled state into the state of C.

Based on the measurement results, Bob's operation typically requires quantum gate operations to convert the entangled state into the correct target state. This complex process involves manipulating quantum states, which requires precise control and measurement techniques. Ultimately, through these operations, Bob can restore the state of the bit to be transmitted (C) without actually transferring the quantum bit C itself. This is one of the critical achievements of QT, allowing the transmission of information without sharing matters.

In this process, Alice and Bob only transmit the measurement results, not the specific bit information to be sent (C). Therefore, even if someone intercepts the communication, they cannot obtain the tip of the bit to be transmitted, as more than the measurement results alone are required. Based on these results, only Alice and Bob know how to manipulate their quantum states to recover the original information.

6.5.2 Transmitting Quantum Information

In 1993, Bennett, Brassard, and four others proposed the teleportation protocol, achieving the transmission of a quantum bit using two classical bit channels and an entangled bit.

In 1997, the Zeilinger group in Austria successfully realized QT communication for the first time. In their experiment, they teleported the quantum state from one photon to another by entangling two photons and measuring one of them. In the same year, Pan Jianwei, then studying in Austria, collaborated with the Dutch researcher Bouwmeester and others to achieve the remote transmission of an unknown quantum state for the first time.

In 2004, the Pan Jianwei group was the first to realize five-photon entanglement and the teleportation of an open quantum state internationally. Subsequently, they achieved the entanglement of six and eight photons. In the same year, a team from the NIST and the University of Innsbruck teleported information encoded in the quantum state of a single atom. Their method involved capturing and entangling two beryllium ions and then teleporting their quantum states over a short distance.

In 2008, scientists from the University of Tokyo teleported quantum information over several kilometers within Tokyo. QT and optical fibers allowed the team to transmit entangled photons over long distances.

In 2011, the first successful free-space QT and entanglement distribution over a hundred kilometers was achieved, solving the long-distance information transmission problem for communication satellites.

In 2015, a group of researchers from NIST transmitted quantum information over 100 km of fiber optic, quadrupling the previous transmission distance.

In 2019, Nanjing University initiated an experiment using drones on air-to-ground quantum entanglement distribution and measurement. The drones, carrying optical transmitters, completed quantum entanglement distribution measurements with ground receiving stations over a distance of 200 m.

Overall, QT provides a better way of transmitting quantum information: it allows the transfer of information between different locations without the need to move the matter that stores the information physically. Additionally, QT enables secure transmission of encryption keys between communication endpoints (Alice and Bob) because any eavesdropper attempting to intercept the communication cannot obtain crucial information. This makes QT a key technology for the future quantum Internet.

Moreover, in remote quantum computing, Alice can transmit her quantum bit to a remote quantum computer to perform computations and then transmit the results back to her. Through QT, secure remote quantum computing is possible without concerns about the computer's trustworthiness.

QT can also be used for quantum secure authentication, verifying the legitimacy of a communication party, which is crucial for applications requiring high security like banking, government agencies, and military communications.

Finally, QT can be used for long-term information preservation. Since the transmission process does not involve the collapse of quantum states, information can be stored in qubits after transmission and retrieved later, ensuring long-term preservation and secure storage of information.

Although still a laboratory phenomenon, QT has shown a promising future with potential innovative applications to meet the growing demands for information security. As quantum technology develops, we may see more applications based on QT.

6.6   Toward a Quantum Internet

Quantum information technologies, including quantum computing and quantum communication, leverage the unique properties of quantum mechanics. One of their long-term development goals is to construct a secure, efficient, and global quantum Internet that integrates quantum computing and communication for numerous innovative applications and services.

6.6.1 Quantum Computers + Quantum Communication

The quantum Internet is a highly secure and efficient form of the Internet that combines quantum computing and quantum communication technologies. In a quantum Internet, these technologies are integrated to enable novel methods of communication and computation.

Guo Guangcan, a professor and doctoral supervisor at the University of Science and Technology of China, an academician of the Chinese Academy of Sciences and the Academy of Sciences for the Developing World, and director of the Key Laboratory of Quantum Information, introduces in his article "The Current Status and Future of Quantum Information Technology" that the basic elements of the quantum Internet include quantum nodes and quantum channels. The quantum Internet integrates information transmission and processing, with quantum nodes for storing and processing quantum information and quantum channels for transmitting quantum information between nodes.

Quantum nodes, crucial for storing, processing, and transmitting quantum information, include universal quantum computers, special-purpose quantum computers, quantum sensors, and quantum key devices. These nodes utilize principles of quantum mechanics for various tasks, such as quantum computing, sensing, and encryption. Quantum channels, employed for transmitting quantum information in the quantum Internet, are realized through transmitting and measuring quantum states, securing the privacy and safety of communication. All nodes in the quantum Internet can be interconnected through quantum entanglement, enabling highly secure and efficient information transmission. Different quantum nodes and channels form various functional quantum Internet systems.

The quantum Internet is about harnessing and distributing quantum effects through a network. While this is highly complex, it is also incredibly powerful.

One of the core contributions of the quantum Internet is providing absolute communication security. Through QKD, the quantum Internet can completely prevent eavesdropping attacks, ensuring the absolute confidentiality of communication. This feature is vital for government, military, financial, and other critical areas of communication.

Traditional Internet communication relies on classical bit-based encryption techniques, which may be vulnerable to computational limitations and therefore pose a potential threat of being cracked. However, the quantum Internet adopts a novel approach based on the principles of quantum mechanics, making communication absolutely secure. This is achieved as follows:

First, QKD technology allows communication parties to generate and share a unique, unstealable quantum key. If any eavesdropping or interference attempts are made, they will trigger the collapse of the quantum state, immediately alerting both parties. This mechanism ensures absolute confidentiality of communication, as even attackers with supercomputers cannot intercept communication contents without detection.

Second, the global interconnectedness of the quantum Internet allows it to meet the strict security standards of the government, military, and financial sectors. These sectors often require highly confidential communication to ensure national security, military secrets, and the safety of financial transactions. The quantum Internet offers an unparalleled way to meet these requirements, not only preventing current encryption algorithms from being cracked but also resisting future threats from quantum computers.

Another important value of the quantum Internet lies in its role in advancing the field of quantum computing. Quantum computing, a cutting-edge technology, uses the properties of quantum superposition and entanglement in qubits to perform certain computations much faster than traditional computers. However, quantum computing requires many qubits and complex quantum operations. Through the quantum Internet, global research institutions, businesses, and individuals can access remote quantum computing resources without building large, expensive quantum computers.

This has tremendous potential for solving complex problems that current supercomputers struggle with. Drug design, materials science, climate simulation, and complex optimization problems are ideal application areas for quantum computing. The quantum Internet will propel research and innovation in these fields, potentially bringing significant breakthroughs for human society.

6.6.2 How Far Are We from a Quantum Internet?

In October 2018, Wehner, Elkouss, and Hanson co-authored a paper in *Science* outlining six potential phases of future quantum Internet development and what users can do at each level. They termed the first phase as Phase 0, where users can receive quantum-generated codes but cannot send or receive quantum information. This type of network is called QKD, which already exists, most notably in China's 2,000 km Beijing–Shanghai Trunk Line.

In Phase 0, any two users can share an encrypted key, but the service provider also knows it. Advancing to Phase 1, any two users can create a private encrypted key known only to them. Users receive and measure quantum states (but do not necessarily involve entangled quantum phenomena).

Phase 2 of the quantum Internet will leverage the powerful phenomenon of entanglement. The initial goal of this phase is to make quantum encryption essentially unbreakable. Any two end-users can obtain entangled states (but cannot store them), forming what is known as an entanglement distribution network.

Starting from Phase 3, storing and exchanging quantum bits will be possible, known as a quantum memory network: Any two end-users can obtain and store entangled quantum bits and transmit quantum information to each other, making it possible to connect quantum computers through the network.

Phases 4 & 5, the quantum computing network stage, will feature mature quantum computers (capable of correcting data transmission errors). These phases aim to achieve various degrees of distributed quantum computing and quantum sensing, applicable to scientific experiments.

Currently, Phase 1 of the quantum Internet is underway. The US's Q-Next has shared quantum states through a 52-mile fiber-optic link, a potential core of a future national quantum Internet. The European Quantum Internet Alliance (QIA) has also had successes, including the first network connecting three quantum processors, with quantum information transmitted through an intermediary node created by the QuTech quantum information institute. The Max Planck Institute (another QIA member) has shared quantum information using single photons.

As work progresses, we are beginning to see glimpses of a quantum Internet. However, discussing a quantum Internet under current technological conditions still seems remote. Before realizing this vision, many technical challenges and engineering problems need addressing.

Besides technical difficulties, standardization is also a challenge for the quantum Internet. The Internet is known for its "rough consensus and running code." Engineers ensure it works and can be replicated across multiple systems before fixing them in place. The Internet Engineering Task Force (IETF) has been the institution ensuring code runs for years. Since the Internet's inception, the IETF has published standards known as "RFCs" (Requests for Comments). These standards define network protocols, ensuring our emails and video chats can be received by others. We will also need RFCs to dictate how quantum computers communicate for a quantum Internet.

Undoubtedly, the value of a quantum Internet is immeasurable. However, objectively, the entire field of quantum information technology is still in its early research stage, with practical applications yet to come.

6.7 The Right Time for Quantum Communication

In recent years, various countries have been gradually undertaking pilot applications of quantum communication. Since the 1990s, the United States was the first to incorporate quantum technology into its national strategy. In 2003, Harvard University in the US established the world's first experimental quantum secure communication network. The European Union also began emphasizing quantum communication research in the 1990s under its Fifth Framework Program for Research and Development. It later conducted QKD network verification through projects like SECCOQC and Swiss Quantum.

Entering the 21st century, countries like Japan, South Korea, and Singapore began to focus on quantum communication. Japan listed quantum communication as a national high-tech development project in 2000, setting a ten-year mid-to-long-term research plan. South Korea and others also heavily invested in scientific research, setting up experimental centers and specialized agencies for quantum communication, aiming for breakthroughs in the field. Despite starting later in quantum communication, China has achieved notable success, leading globally in pilot application numbers and network construction scale, with many of its construction records surpassing others worldwide. China is the only country directly competing with the US in quantum communication, with a leading advantage in this area, while the US holds an advantage in quantum computing.

6.7.1 The Industrialization Path of Quantum Communication

In terms of quantum communication pilot applications, the US started earliest. By the end of the 20th century, the US government identified quantum information as a key support subject in its "Maintaining National Competitiveness" program. The US NIST designated quantum information as one of its three main research directions. With government support, the industrialization of quantum communication in the US developed rapidly.

In 1989, IBM successfully conducted the world's first quantum information transmission experiment in a laboratory at a transmission rate of 10 bps, although the distance was only 32 m. In 2003, the US Defense Advanced Research Projects Agency established the DARPA Quantum Communication Network between BBN Laboratories, Harvard University, and Boston University, the world's first quantum cryptographic communication network. Initially, the network had 6 QKD nodes, later expanding to 10, with the farthest communication distance reaching 29 km.

Subsequently, the US, Europe, Japan, and other regions successively established several quantum communication experimental networks, such as Swiss Quantum, Tokyo QKD, and Vienna SECOQC, demonstrating applications like metropolitan networking, quantum telephony, and secure communication of infrastructure.

Core technologies of global quantum communication companies mainly originate from universities and research institutions. In the US, companies like MagiQ (founded by MIT) and Qubitekk (established by Los Alamos National Laboratory) provide comprehensive quantum information security encryption solutions and have deployed application promotion services in defense and power grid infrastructure. They also hold strong capabilities and reserves in patents and intellectual property in quantum communication.

In Europe, university-incubated startups like IDQ (founded by the University of Geneva) and AIT (established by the University of Vienna) have years of technical accumulation in QKD research and diversified development in technology routes and industry applications. They have deeply engaged in the commercial application of QKD for many years, gaining extensive market promotion experience.

Additionally, research institutions and enterprises like Toshiba in Japan, the Cambridge Research Laboratory in the UK, and InfiniQuant in Germany are active in technology and application research. They possess key technologies in integration and chipization, have high market competitiveness, and play a major role in standardizing QKD technology.

In 2016, Battelle built a 650 km quantum secure communication fiber line from Ohio to Washington and initiated a plan for a nationwide quantum communication backbone network for demonstrative applications in the US. Using Swiss IDQ equipment, the network aims to provide quantum security services for communication between companies like Google, IBM, Microsoft, and Amazon data centers. In 2018, Quantum Xchange announced a plan to build an 805 km commercial QKD line between Washington and Boston. In 2022, Florida Atlantic University, Qubitekk, and US defense contractor L3Harris collaborated to develop the first drone-based mobile quantum communication network for the US Air Force.

In Europe, countries like Italy and Spain are starting to build QKD networks and applications of quantum secure encryption. For instance, in June 2018, Spain's Telefonica, Huawei, and the Technical University of Madrid innovatively conducted an SDN-based QKD metropolitan network demonstration experiment. The EU plans to establish a pan-European quantum secure Internet around 2035.

In 2014, the UK began constructing quantum secure experimental networks in London, Cambridge, Bristol, etc., under its "National Quantum Technology Program," aiming to build a nationwide practical quantum secure communication line within ten years, connecting internationally to form a global quantum secure communication network.

In Asia, Japan and Europe jointly established the Tokyo Quantum Secure Communication Testbed Network in 2010, with continuous live network trials by multiple research institutions. NTT, Toshiba, and others drive QKD research and applications, offering secure encryption services in government and medical fields. In 2015, South Korea's SKT announced plans to build a star-shaped quantum secure communication network connecting Bundang, Suwon, and Seoul, spanning around 256 km, aiming to establish a nationwide network by 2025 to promote quantum secure encryption services.

6.7.2 China's Quantum Communication: A Late Bloomer Leading the Way

China may not have been the earliest in quantum communication, but it has developed rapidly. With major projects like the "Quantum Satellite" and the "Beijing–Shanghai Trunk Line," China's quantum communication technology has reached a global leading position.

China's rapid progress in quantum communication is inseparable from early national planning and support. As early as 2013, China proactively deployed the world's first long-distance quantum secure communication line, the "Beijing–Shanghai Trunk Line," pioneering related technology applications and gaining valuable experience. To maintain its leading position in the industrialization of quantum secure communication, national and local governments, and departments have given high priority and support to quantum secure communication in recent years.

In 2015, General Secretary Xi Jinping explicitly pointed out in his "13th Five-Year Plan" explanation that major scientific and technological projects reflecting national strategic intentions should be deployed in fields such as quantum communication. The quantum information industry has become strategically nurtured in the 13th Five-Year Plan. As a national strategic industry, the development of the quantum communication industry has been supported by national strategies, technological leadership, industrial promotion, engineering construction, and more, appearing in important national plans such as the 13th Five-Year Plan for National Economic and Social Development and the 13th Five-Year National Strategic Emerging Industries Development Plan. The National Development and Reform Commission (NDRC) also listed the phase I project of the National Wide-Area Quantum Secure Communication Backbone Network as one of the proposed support projects for the new generation of information infrastructure construction in 2018.

Regional governments directly support the development of quantum technology and the construction of quantum secure communication networks through government documents. Many provinces, including Anhui, Shandong, Beijing, Shanghai, Jiangsu, Zhejiang, Guangdong, and Xinjiang, have incorporated the development of quantum information technology and the construction of quantum communication networks into their 2018 government work reports and promoted implementation. Particularly, the construction of quantum secure intercity trunk lines in the Yangtze River Delta urban agglomeration was included in the 13th Five-Year Plan.

In the newly released Outline of the Integrated Development Plan for the Yangtze River Delta Region in 2019, quantum information has become a key industry for future planning and layout in the Yangtze River Delta. From a local policy perspective, governments in Guiyang, Haikou, Zaozhuang, Kunming, Guangzhou, Jinhua, Nanjing, and other places have also introduced policies to support the construction of quantum communication networks. After the release of the Shandong Province Quantum Technology Innovation Development Plan (2018–2025), the Several Policies and Measures of the Jinan Municipal People's Government on Accelerating the Construction of Quantum Information Science Center became the first specialized policy for the quantum information industry in China, laying a solid foundation for local development.

China currently maintains a leading advantage in the field of quantum communication, mainly manifested in technological breakthroughs and industrial construction.

From a technological breakthrough perspective, on August 16, 2016, China launched the world's first quantum science experimental satellite, Micius, enabling humanity to conduct quantum science experiments on a spatial scale for the first time. It exceeded expectations in completing three major scientific tasks in 2017: absolutely secure QKD between satellite and ground, verification of space Bell inequalities, and realization of invisible teleportation between ground and satellite. The research team led by Pan Jianwei from the University of Science and Technology of China (USTC) was awarded the 2018 Cleveland Prize for this achievement. China was the first international country to successfully achieve thousand-kilometer-level star-to-ground two-way QKD using the Micius quantum satellite and the first to achieve quantum invisible teleportation from satellite to ground. This laid a solid scientific and technological foundation for China to continue leading the development of world quantum communication technology and at the forefront of research on basic quantum physics problems on a spatial scale.

In September 2017, China took the lead in completing the "Beijing–Shanghai Trunk Line," opening the world's first quantum secure communication trunk line. China was also the first country to deploy a large-scale quantum secure communication network; since the construction of the Beijing–Shanghai Trunk Line, it has been connected to the Micius quantum science experimental satellite, forming the embryonic form of an integrated sky-to-ground quantum communication network, marking China's entry into the wide-area network stage.

In terms of industrial construction, the first step was taken in May 2009, when Pan Jianwei and Peng Chengzhi's team established Anhui Quantum Communication Co., Ltd. (the predecessor of USTC Quantum), with technology originating from the Hefei National Laboratory for Physical Sciences at the Microscale. In July of the same year, relying on the CAS Key Laboratory of Quantum Information, Guo Guangcan and Han Zhengfu's team established QSKY Tech in Wuhu, Anhui. Both companies engage in the quantum secure communication business.

Upon its establishment, Anhui Quantum participated in constructing the "quantum secure communication hotline" for the 60th National Day military parade. In September 2011, QuantumCTek's first-generation GHz high-speed QKD product was launched. It now possesses core equipment for quantum secure communication networks, including QKD and channel and key network exchange products. These products are deployed in quantum secure communication backbone networks, metropolitan area networks, and industry-specific access networks.

In 2012, Anhui Quantum participated in the construction of multiple projects, including the Hefei Metropolitan Quantum Communication Experimental Demonstration Network, Xinhua News Agency Financial Information Quantum Communication Verification Network, and the 18th National Congress Quantum Secure Communication Security. In 2014, the company was renamed USTC QuantumCTek on its fifth anniversary.

QSKY is also a leader in the field of quantum communication. In 2010, the company's development and production of infrared single-photon detectors achieved mass production, making China the third country globally capable of mass-producing infrared single-photon detectors.

After a decade of exploration and practice, QuantumCTek and QSKY have grown into global leaders in quantum communication equipment manufacturing and quantum security solution providers, with nearly all of China's quantum secure communication construction related to these two companies. QuantumCTek has grown into China's first listed quantum communication company.

With technological advancements, Jiuzhou Quantum and ZCWEI Quantum were established in Zhejiang and Beijing between 2012 and 2014.

Following the successful launch of the world's first quantum science experimental satellite "Micuis" in 2016, quantum communication became a popular industry. That year, the National Innovation-Driven Development Strategy listed quantum information technology as a disruptive technology leading to industrial transformation. The "China Quantum Communication Industry Alliance," jointly initiated by the Chinese Academy of Sciences, USTC, QuantumCTek, Alibaba, ZTE, and other institutions, was also established in Beijing.

That same year, Pan Jianwei and Peng Chengzhi's team established CAS Quantum Network Co., Ltd. in Shanghai, a state-owned holding company jointly invested by the Chinese Academy of Sciences and USTC. The NDRC approves it and undertakes the strategic task of building and operating the national wide-area quantum communication network. Simply put, CAS Quantum Network and QuantumCTek have a relationship between an operator and an equipment manufacturer.

That year, Chen Liuping, former chief engineer of MagiQ, established Qudoor Quantum in Beijing. With over 20 years of experience in quantum communication and quantum computing, Qudoor Quantum has independently developed quantum communication terminals, network switching/routing, optoelectronic core devices, quantum control, and application software. It provides quantum security protection in government, defense, finance, power, energy, and big data fields.

Although quantum communication is still in its early stages, China's quantum communication industry chain has become increasingly complete. The upstream of the industry chain mainly consists of core equipment manufacturers like QuantumCTek, QSKY, and Jiuzhou Quantum, the most critical link in the quantum secure communication industry chain. Core equipment includes QKD devices, quantum switches, quantum gateways, quantum network station control, quantum random number generators, etc. Quantum secure communication also utilizes classical channels, so telecommunications equipment manufacturers like Huawei and ZTE are also part of the industry chain.

It can be said that for a long time, China's scientific research has been more of a follower, but quantum communication is one of the few areas where China has achieved a "from 0 to 1" breakthrough in basic research and leads the world. This also represents an important opportunity for China to take the lead in cutting-edge technological fields.

Part 3

The Quantum Age in Flux

"QUANTUMIZED" MATERIALS

7.1 The Quantum Mysteries behind Semiconductors

One of the major accomplishments of quantum mechanics is bridging the gap between physics and chemistry, expanding the boundaries of human understanding of the world, especially in the realm of materials.

It's well-known that advancements in materials have largely driven technological progress, and our understanding of materials reflects our comprehension of the world. Since the Renaissance, modern scientists have embarked on scientific explorations, synthesizing and processing new materials, from plastics to contemporary graphene and carbon nanotubes. The recognition and discovery of materials have been integral throughout the history of modern scientific development.

The breakthroughs in quantum theory have also brought new directions to materials, among which semiconductors, born from quantum mechanics, stand as one of the most vital. It's hard to imagine modern life without semiconductors: no computers, mobile phones, or digital cameras. If we reverted to the era of vacuum tubes, radios would be larger than microwaves.

7.1.1 Understanding Semiconductors from a Quantum Perspective

Semiconductor technology forms the foundation of all integrated circuits. Nowadays, semiconductors are widely used in our daily lives—the smartphones in our hands, the televisions in our homes, and the computers we use regularly. Without quantum mechanics, no one would have thought such devices could function.

What exactly is a semiconductor? We know that electrons exist in atoms and under certain conditions, they can break free from atomic nuclei and move freely within some materials, creating an electric current. We can imagine moving electrons as cars and the materials they pass through as roads. The size of the electric current, or how fast the cars run, depends on the road conditions. Materials with good road conditions where cars can run fast without significant obstacles are known as conductors.

Most metals, such as copper, aluminum, and iron, are conductors. However, some materials have poor road conditions full of obstacles, where cars get stuck and can't move at all. These materials are called insulators. Common insulators include ceramics, rubber, and glass.

Then, there are special materials with peculiar road conditions. Generally, cars would get stuck on these roads, but if external conditions change, such as an increase in temperature, the cars can start moving. These special materials are semiconductors, and the phenomena they exhibit are based on principles of quantum mechanics.

We understand that matter is composed of atoms, and according to quantum mechanics, the electrons in a material are like being in a large box where they can move freely. For instance, in a silicon single-crystal cube, its internal electrons can freely move within this cubic box. If they hit the walls of the box, they bounce back. Therefore, in quantum mechanics, particles within a box generally do not have a definite position and can appear anywhere inside the box; however, their energy is often more definite, as particles tend to move toward the lowest energy state.

Here, quantum mechanics can easily calculate the definite energy states of the electrons in the box, i.e., the energy eigenstates. Due to the wave-particle duality of quantum mechanics, these energy eigenstates are standing waves reflecting back and forth between the box's walls, with wavelengths only taking certain specific values. To an extent, it can be understood that electrons constantly hit the walls and walk back and forth, but their speed is inversely proportional to the wavelength and can only be an integral multiple of a basic unit.

As a result, the energy of the particles can only take a series of discrete values. Each of these energy eigenstates is called an energy level. However, when the box becomes large enough to accommodate many electrons, these energy levels become very dense, almost continuous, but still not infinitely many.

Thus, from an energy perspective, electrons form a deep ocean. Below a certain energy level, all the energy levels are filled. But a body is not always in the lowest energy state, as there is internal thermal motion. For electrons, thermal motion means that the surface electrons change state, perhaps jumping to a slightly higher energy level, similar to ripples and waves on the ocean surface. As for the deeper electrons, they still can't move as the slightly higher and lower energy levels are all occupied, and thermal motion doesn't have enough energy to knock them above sea level.

Similarly, if an external force, such as voltage, is used in a material, only the surface electrons can drift with the electric field to form an electric current. Although all electrons should be considered shared by all atoms, only a minimal number of electrons on the ocean's surface are truly free. In contrast, the electrons deep in the ocean generally can't move under normal circumstances. However, there are special cases, such as when a high-energy particle from cosmic rays enters, it can knock out many deep electrons, creating many free electrons along the way.

When a free electron encounters a deep, unfree electron, nothing usually happens under normal circumstances. This is very different from the classical mechanics scenario. In classical mechanics, two electrons in the same space repel each other, and they definitely have a non-zero probability of colliding or exchanging energy. In quantum mechanics, however, although the interaction between electrons always exists, such interaction requires conditions to produce consequences. Collisions of particles in the same space are not destined to happen. This is why, in some materials, once an electric current is formed, it doesn't stop; the current doesn't decay due to collisions with other particles inside the material, which is the case with superconductors. Deep electrons do influence free electrons, resembling transparent clouds of charge; their presence affects the distribution of the electric field within the material.

Looking at atomic nuclei, although electrons can drift freely, the atomic nuclei, thousands of times heavier, are difficult to move. The study of quantum physics in solids starts with crystals, where atomic nuclei are arranged in a periodic and orderly manner. A more refined physical model is that atomic nuclei are nailed at lattice points, and all atomic nuclei share electrons. Inside a crystal, due to the attraction of atomic nuclei, electrons are naturally more likely to be close to atomic nuclei. But more importantly, in crystals, electron energy levels are no longer near continuous but split into many energy bands from top to bottom. Within each energy band, energy levels are still very densely close to continuous, but there are gaps between different energy bands, called band gaps. No energy levels exist in the band gaps.

The electron energy ocean is now divided into many layers, but except for the top layer, all the oceans are fully filled and won't produce an electric current. The top energy band is only partially filled in some materials, leaving some free electrons on the ocean's surface that can conduct electricity. These are the so-called conductors, including all metallic materials. The top energy band is filled in other materials, with no free electrons inside. Above that is an empty energy band, but the electric field strength produced by applying a voltage to the material is insufficient to make electrons jump up there. Such materials are insulators.

Semiconductors, like insulators, have their top energy bands filled and basically don't conduct electricity at very low temperatures. However, their band gaps are relatively narrow, and thermal motion can cause a few electrons to jump into the empty energy band above, becoming completely free electrons. The number of free electrons that jump up increases exponentially with the increase in the band gap, meaning that a slight increase in the band gap can reduce the number of free electrons by thousands to millions of times. Therefore, the transition from an insulator to a semiconductor is an example of a qualitative change caused by quantitative changes.

7.1.2 PN Junctions and MOS Transistors

It's evident that semiconductor technology is fundamentally rooted in band theory derived from quantum mechanics, specifically the solid-state band theory and some key conclusions of quantum mechanics.

When a few thermal electrons jump to the upper energy band (conduction band) and gain freedom in semiconductor materials, the lower energy band (valence band) also has some vacant energy levels. Such vacancies are called holes. With holes present, the valence band can also conduct electricity. An electric current is essentially an imbalance of electron movement in one direction over another. Vacancies allow electrons to adjust their states in response to an external electric field, generating an electric current.

In pure semiconductor materials, electrons and holes are always generated in pairs in equal numbers. Introducing impurities into the material can alter this balance. Some impurities contribute holes, creating P-type semiconductors with more holes; others contribute extra free electrons, resulting in N-type semiconductors with an abundance of free electrons.

Very interesting physical effects occur at this interface when a P-type semiconductor is placed in close contact with an N-type semiconductor. Such a structure is called a PN junction, which has numerous applications and is essentially the foundation of all semiconductor devices.

When you pour a spoonful of salt into a bucket of water, the salt diffuses until it's evenly distributed—a basic law of statistical physics stating that particles always move from areas of high concentration to areas of low concentration. Therefore, if adjacent areas of the same silicon slice are doped with P-type and N-type impurities, the high concentration of holes in the P region will cause them to diffuse into the N region; similarly, the high concentration of free electrons in the N region will cause them to diffuse into the P region.

When electrons and holes meet, they recombine, filling the vacant spots and neutralizing each other. At the interface between the P and N regions, a layer forms where both electrons and holes disappear, known as the depletion layer. However, this diffusion doesn't continue indefinitely. The P region, initially electrically neutral, becomes negatively charged due to the loss of some holes in the depletion layer, attracting holes to prevent them from continuing to leave. Similarly, the N region becomes positively charged. An electric field forms in the depletion layer, pushing holes toward the P region and electrons toward the N region, eventually reaching an equilibrium. The thickness of the depletion layer is typically on the order of micrometers or even thinner, with higher doping concentrations resulting in thinner depletion layers.

A key characteristic of the PN junction is its unidirectional conductivity. The established equilibrium is disrupted if a positive voltage is applied to the P region and a negative voltage to the N region. The positive voltage creates more holes that rush toward the depletion region, and the negative voltage's free electrons also move toward the depletion region, thinning it out. Continuous recombination of holes and electrons in this area forms an electric current, which is the forward direction of the PN junction.

If the direction of the voltage is reversed, both holes and electrons move away from the depletion region, thickening it until carriers are depleted, and no electric current can flow. This is the reverse direction of the PN junction.

Based on the PN junction, physicists at Bell Labs, including Bardeen, invented the transistor, earning them the 1956 Nobel Prize in Physics. The invention of the transistor initiated the miniaturization of electronic devices, leading to today's ultra-large-scale integrated circuits and ushering human society into the information age.

The field-effect transistor (FET) is the most common type in integrated circuit chips. Although initially invented for signal amplification, FETs are primarily used as switches in today's digital age, controlled by voltage. Every digital chip consists of numerous such switches.

A FET has three terminals, and the substrate requires a power supply. The source and drain terminals are connected to a high-concentration N-type doped region on the P-type semiconductor substrate. The high-concentration doping regions conduct electricity well, and the contact between the semiconductor and metal terminals is excellent. These two terminals and the substrate each form a PN junction. In practical use, the P-type substrate is connected to zero potential, and the potentials at the source and drain are always positive. Thus, both PN junctions are reverse-biased and non-conductive. We do not want current to leak from the terminals into the substrate. The source and drain, separated by two reverse-biased PN junctions without the gate's influence, are non-conductive.

The gate functions as a switch made of metal or conductive material. Between the gate and the silicon substrate, there is a layer of insulating silicon dioxide to prevent current leakage to the substrate. When a high voltage is applied to the gate, the positively charged holes underneath are repelled, attracting the minority free electrons in the material.

Once the voltage exceeds a critical value, the thin layer beneath the gate is no longer a P-type semiconductor but reverses to an N-type region. This N-type reversed region is called the channel, connecting the source and drain N regions, allowing conductivity between the source and drain. This type of FET is called a MOSFET, named after the structure beneath the gate: Metal-Oxide-Semiconductor. This MOSFET, with an N-type channel for conduction, is also known as an NMOS transistor. The NMOS transistor is characterized by conduction when the gate is at a high potential and closure at a low potential.

The physical core of semiconductor electronic devices differs among various devices but generally involves PN junctions and MOS transistors. Therefore, utilizing the properties of semiconductors, useful electronic components can be created, with diodes and transistors being the most important.

Diodes have a unique property: when voltage is applied in one direction, they produce an electric current, but when voltage is applied in the opposite direction, no current flows. This is akin to one-way streets in a city: you can drive in one direction but not the other. Diodes can act as switches in circuits.

LEDs, or Light light-emitting diodes, are a special type of diode that emits light. The inventors of LEDs, Akasaki Isamu, Amano Hiroshi, and Nakamura Shuji, won the Nobel Prize in Physics in 2014. LEDs are significantly more efficient than incandescent bulbs, making them very energy-efficient. This is why many stores, like IKEA, sell light bulbs made of LEDs. Their long lifespan, over ten times that of incandescent bulbs, is another advantage, leading many to believe that LEDs will be the mainstream light source of the future.

7.2 Two-Dimensional Quantum Mechanics and Graphene

To date, quantum mechanics has mostly been applied in three-dimensional contexts, such as in quantum measurement, quantum communication, quantum computing, and semiconductors. However, quantum theory also has significant implications in two-dimensional spaces, with graphene being the most representative material in this realm.

7.2.1 Understanding Graphene from a Quantum Perspective

Plastics, one of the greatest inventions of the 20th century, began with John Wesley Hyatt's discovery in 1869 that adding camphor to nitrocellulose created a flexible and rigid material named Celluloid, the oldest plastic product. Initially used for billiard balls and film stock, it marked the birth of the plastic industry.

The true explosion in plastics usage came with Leo Baekeland's 1907 invention of Bakelite, laying the foundation for various plastics, permeating into telephones, radios, firearms, coffeepots, jewelry, and even the first atomic bomb. If the invention of plastics was the 20th century's greatest material breakthrough, graphene could well be the 21st century's revolutionary material. Graphene's transformative power is no less than that of early plastics.

Graphene, like plastics, is composed of carbon-based molecules. On October 5, 2010, the Royal Swedish Academy of Sciences awarded Andre Geim and Konstantin Novoselov the Nobel Prize in Physics for isolating graphene and discovering its extraordinary properties, showcasing the wonders of quantum physics.

Graphene's theoretical research dates back just over 60 years and was once considered a hypothetical structure that couldn't exist independently. Common graphite is made of millions of graphene layers stacked together. A pencil stroke on paper could leave a trace of one or more graphene layers. Graphite layers easily separate into thin flakes, and further thinning these flakes to a single carbon atom's thickness yields graphene.

Based on this principle, physicists Andre Geim and Konstantin Novoselov at the University of Manchester successfully isolated graphene from graphite in 2004 using mechanical exfoliation. This two-dimensional carbon material, tightly packed in a benzene ring structure, is the fundamental building block of other graphite materials, capable of forming zero-dimensional fullerenes (buckyballs), one-dimensional carbon nanotubes, and three-dimensional graphite.

Graphene's most famous and magical attribute is its two-dimensional nature. Though it has a thickness, it's only as thick as a single carbon atom, with any more or less disqualifying it as graphene. Adding a layer of carbon atoms transforms it into graphite, and removing a layer leaves nothing. Graphene's discovery not only shattered the traditional notion that two-dimensional materials couldn't exist in nature but also significantly enriched the carbon material family, paving the way for transforming traditional industries and fostering the rapid emergence of strategic new industries.

Graphene's extraordinary characteristics stem from its unique structure—it appears as a black powder to the naked eye, seemingly weightless. Yet, it's the best-known conductor of electricity and heat, lightest, strongest, toughest, highly transparent, and has a high surface area. With excellent optical, electrical, thermal, and mechanical properties, graphene's potential applications are boundless, earning it the moniker "black gold" of the carbon era.

At its core, graphite has a layered structure. Each layer forms a honeycomb network of hexagons, with 0.14 nm between adjacent atoms within a layer and 0.34 nm between layers. The bond between layers is weak, making graphite soft and easily flaking into fine powder, ideal for pencil leads.

Diamond and graphite, both carbon-based, are different allotropes, vividly demonstrating that a substance's properties depend not only on its constituent atoms but also on its crystal structure. Diamonds are prized for their unique crystalline formation under high-pressure, high-temperature conditions deep within the earth.

For graphene, the question arises: how can four-valent carbon atoms form a hexagonal crystal? This is closely related to covalent bonds, particularly the π bond. High school chemistry introduces benzene, a ring molecule formed by six carbon and six hydrogen atoms, featuring a π bond. Benzene's structure requires four lines from each carbon atom. Similarly, the crystal network of graphene can be depicted in the figure. However, this representation is oversimplified, with seemingly asymmetric single and double bonds. The π bond unites the carbon atom rings into perfectly symmetrical hexagons.

(a) Benzene

(c) Benzene

(b) Graphene

This simplistic image can be slightly refined: benzene has two possible structures, with each carbon atom choosing to form a double bond with either of its two adjacent carbon atoms. The actual benzene molecule is a quantum superposition of these two possibilities, and for graphene, it's a superposition of three possibilities.

7.2.2 The Promise of a New Material: Graphene

It is well-known that materials form the foundation for human survival and development, driving the evolution of human civilization. From wood, stone, and mud to copper, iron, steel, silicon chips, and carbon fiber, history shows that each new era of human society is marked by the emergence of new material, often becoming the "engine" of productivity in that era. However, all past materials couldn't escape the fate of degradation over time due to wear and tear.

For example, denim jeans thin out and even tear with prolonged wear; kitchen blenders eventually break down as gears used for adjusting motor speed and mixing intensity wear out; and cars become unusable due to aging transmissions. Over time, friction causes wear and tear, naturally leading to the failure of the transmission system.

The fundamental reason for material degradation is the presence of friction. When two surfaces rub against each other, the actual contact points are only nanometers in size, involving friction between just a few atoms. The reasons behind friction are complex, encompassing surface roughness, minor shape changes in the material, and surface contamination. The energy generated between moving surfaces during friction is converted into heat, leading to potentially destructive outcomes.

For instance, the heat generated by the friction of moving parts within a car engine and during driving is the primary reason for using motor oil and cooling systems. Without lubrication and cooling, the heat from the engine would quickly destroy it and could even cause the car to catch fire.

However, graphene perfectly addresses the past material defects caused by friction. Graphene coatings are applied to small mechanical parts, significantly enhancing their lifespan and almost eliminating the ineffective heat generated by friction.

Moreover, selective impurities can be added to graphene coatings for atomic-level calibration when applied to micro-mechanical devices. This allows for completely avoiding friction in the desired direction of motion while enabling friction in other directions. This passive self-calibration solution has been tested in laboratories.

Beyond its low friction, graphene also holds another revolutionary application value: its super high strength. One method to enhance strength and fracture resistance in various products is to increase their volume: thickening plastic or wood to prevent breakage, increasing material density for strength, or adding beams or fixtures to share the stress during use. These solutions all have a common side effect—increasing the object's weight while enhancing strength. This raises the question whether people will add weight for drop protection features.

Using denser materials in certain hardware enhances safety for cars, but the added weight reduces fuel economy. However, we can use graphene instead of traditional reinforcement methods to make objects stronger and lighter. Graphene can improve their durability from car engines and tires that have not sustained actual damage to mechanical equipment that doesn't require frequent maintenance due to everyday wear and tear.

Finally, and most anticipated, is graphene's "lightweight and flexible" characteristic. Composed of a single layer of atoms arranged in a plane, graphene is ultra-thin and extremely strong. This means graphene can be bent, curled, and folded into any imaginable shape. Graphene materials can stretch up to 120% of their original size without breaking and easily return to their initial state. Additionally, graphene can transmit 92% of the visible light projected onto it. In other words, graphene is lightweight, flexible, conductive, and almost invisible.

This lays the foundation for future smart devices. For example, film computers made of graphene can cover car windows covertly, providing maps and real-time traffic reports for cars soon to feature autonomous driving and help drivers choose the best routes between any two locations. Applications of graphene sheets also include micro-embedded computers that can integrate with contact lenses. In the future, people could use heads-up display technology to have information they need to look up displayed right before their eyes.

Looking ahead, if the potential of graphene is fully realized, significant break-throughs in cutting-edge fields like big data, the IoT, cloud computing, and smart devices are imminent, not only achieving "interconnectivity of all things" but also completely overturning the production and lifestyle habits people have grown accustomed to.

7.2.3 How Far Is the "Black Gold" Era?

Currently, graphene is poetically described as "black gold," "the universal material," "king of new materials," "future material," and "revolutionary material." Some scien-tists even predict it could trigger a disruptive technological revolution worldwide, radically transforming the 21st century. However, graphene remains somewhat distant from the average consumer. Besides common barriers in manufacturing, marketing, and distribution of new or modified products, graphene faces additional challenges such as establishing and maintaining raw material supply chains, com-peting against technologies with solid customer bases, and navigating inevitable legal issues.

The main reasons for these challenges are twofold. First, the manufacturing of graphene still faces hurdles. Currently, there are four main methods for producing graphene: mechanical exfoliation, chemical vapor deposition, epitaxial growth on silicon carbide (SiC), and the reduction of graphene oxide. Each of these methods has its own strengths and limitations, affecting the feasibility and quality of graph-ene production.

Fortunately, as companies worldwide join the graphene production ranks, new methods for producing graphene continue to emerge at an astonishing rate. It seems plausible that we may see large-scale graphene production within a few years. Some companies may still focus on small-scale, customized graphene production (e.g., producing graphene sheets ranging from millimeters to centimeters in length), which are useful as additives or combined with other materials. Annual graphene production needs to exceed thousands of tons for practical and profitable use.

Second, before widespread application, graphene must meet market expec-tations by offering higher benefits or lower costs than existing technologies. Addi-tionally, it needs to ensure a bulk supply of quality material within specified time frames. Faced with thousands of new graphene application patents filed annually, the current global graphene production barely meets the needs of laboratory researchers and the commercial market, making high-quality graphene products quite expensive.

However, if a "killer application" based on graphene is invented, it could trigger a race for mass production to meet this demand. Once production scales up, especially with multiple suppliers, the cost per unit of graphene will decrease, allowing for a robust commercial market.

Industrial history shows that the invention of new materials plays a crucial role in modern industry, often spawning new industries or even clusters of industries. However, the industrialization of new materials typically involves significant uncertainties in technology, market, and organization. If we consider the silicon material industry's maturity cycle of 20 years as a benchmark, graphene's industrial maturity is still five to ten years away. Therefore, there's still some distance to cover for graphene to lead the "black gold" era truly.

7.3 Quantum Mechanics Takes the Stage in Technology

Though born in the microscopic world and primarily describing it, quantum mechanics has now intermingled and developed with disciplines such as nuclear science, informatics, and materials science, spurring a quantum technological revolution. Entering the 21st century, applications of quantum mechanics in computing, communication, and measurement are increasingly abundant. Numerous technologies have been widely adopted and significantly advanced societal progress. We are accelerating into an era dominated by quantum technology.

7.3.1 The First Wave of Quantum Technology

We know that quanta are the fundamental units that makeup matter, representing indivisible microscopic particles like photons and electrons. Quantum mechanics studies and describes the structure, properties, and interactions of these basic particles in the microscopic world, forming, along with relativity, the two foundational theories of modern physics.

In the mid-20th century, with the flourishing development of quantum mechanics, the first wave of quantum technology arose, represented by modern optics, electronics, and condensed matter physics. This wave birthed epoch-making technological breakthroughs like lasers, semiconductors, and atomic energy, laying the foundation for the formation and development of the modern information society.

For instance, we often see advertisements for laser beauty treatments, claiming that lasers can remove spots and unwanted hair. This utilizes principles related to quantum mechanics. We know matter is composed of atoms with a nucleus surrounded by electrons moving in fixed orbits, each with different energy levels.

Like any light, lasers consist of photons, each with a certain amount of energy. The energy of photons in common light sources, like sunlight, varies. However, lasers are unique; each photon in a laser has the same amount of energy, distinguishing lasers from ordinary light.

When a laser hits the skin, if the energy of electrons in the skin doesn't match the laser photons' energy, the laser won't be absorbed. Conversely, if they match, the laser will be absorbed, destroying the targeted area. This is the principle behind laser treatments.

Limited by insufficient observation and manipulation capabilities of microscopic physical systems, the first wave of quantum technology brought many exciting applications. However, its main technological feature was understanding and utilizing microscopic physical laws like energy level transitions, stimulated radiation, and chain reactions, while observations and manipulations remained at the macroscopic level.

Fast forward to the 21st century, with deeper understanding, research, and control over quantum mechanics and microscopic physical systems, the second wave of quantum technology is emerging. This wave is on the brink of arrival, characterized by precise observation and manipulation of microscopic particle systems and utilizing unique quantum mechanical features like superposition and entanglement states.

The evolution of quantum technology promises to change and enhance human capabilities in acquiring, transmitting, and processing information, offering a powerful impetus for the future evolution and development of the information society. Integrating with communication, computing, and sensing measurements in informatics, Quantum technology is forming a new field of quantum information technology.

Current applications of quantum technology in quantum computing, communication, and measurement show the potential to break through classical technological limitations in processing speed, information security, measurement precision, and sensitivity. Quantum information technology has become a focal point in the evolution and upgrading of information and communication technology, poised to have foundational and even revolutionary impacts on future national technological development, emerging industries, defense, and economic construction.

7.3.2 Leading the Next Generation of Technological Revolution

Today, the acceleration of emerging information technologies like AI, quantum information technology, blockchain, and 5G is driving humanity's transition from a material-based to a knowledge-based society. In this knowledge era, the importance of information is surpassing that of physical matter, becoming humanity's most valuable strategic resource. The demand for information has reached unprecedented heights, and traditional technologies based on classical physics can no longer meet the requirements for information acquisition, transmission, and processing. This has led to three major technological dilemmas.

First, computing power is approaching its limit. In the era of big data, while the amount of data humans obtain is exploding, the immense volume of data is constrained by traditional storage space. Additionally, the development of AI technology demands higher computing power. However, the computational ability of traditional computers, limited by Moore's Law, struggles to keep pace. Although supercomputing can be achieved through hardware stacking, its capacity for computational improvement is minimal and consumes a vast amount of energy.

Second, information security is an ongoing battle. Traditional encryption technologies are built on computational complexity. However, such encryption systems can theoretically be cracked as computing power increases. Even blockchain, built on computational power, is not immune to these vulnerabilities, leaving gaps and risks in information security.

Third, achieving precision in information is increasingly challenging. Traditional classical measurement tools can no longer meet humanity's demands for accuracy. Many applications require more precise measurements, such as time standards, medical diagnostics, navigation, signal detection, and scientific research, calling for new technologies to break through the current developmental impasse.

In response to these challenges posed by current information technology, quantum technology based on quantum mechanics shows unique advantages, offering new solutions to break through the bottlenecks of traditional classical technology.

First, quantum computers will break the bottleneck of computational power. Quantum computing, using qubits as the basic unit and controlled evolution of quantum states, achieves data storage and computation with unparalleled information-carrying and parallel processing capabilities compared to classical computing. The leap in computational power from quantum computing technology could act as a "catalyst" for future technological evolution. Once breakthroughs are achieved, they could disrupt many socio-economic fields, including basic research, new material and pharmaceutical development, information security, and AI, playing a significant role in national technological development and industrial transformation and upgrading.

Second, quantum communication will break the bottleneck of communication security. The quantum states of microscopic particles are unclonable, meaning any attempt to steal information will disrupt the original information and be detected by the receiver. Thus, quantum communication ensures absolute security from a physical principle level. Quantum communication, ensuring information or key transmission security, mainly includes QT and QKD. Research and development in quantum communication and quantum information networks will bring significant changes and impacts in information security and communication networks, becoming a focal point of technological development and evolution in the future information and communication industry.

Last, quantum precision measurement will break the bottleneck of measurement accuracy. Quantum precision measurement technology can achieve a leap in measurement accuracy compared to traditional measurement techniques. Quantum measurement, based on precise measurement of microscopic particle systems and their quantum states, outperforms traditional measurement techniques in terms of precision, sensitivity, and stability. This includes time standards, inertial measurement, gravity measurement, magnetic field measurement, and target identification, widely applied in basic research, space exploration, biomedical, inertial guidance, geological survey, disaster prevention, and more. Quantum physical constants and quantum measurement technology have become important references for defining basic physical unit measurements, and future quantum measurements are expected to find early applications in biological research, medical diagnostics, and new-generation PNT systems for aerospace, defense, and commercial uses.

With continuous scientific and technological progress, quantum technology will lead a new wave of technological revolution and gradually impact all aspects of societal development, propelling humanity into the era of quantum civilization.

7.3.3 Rapid Development of Quantum Science

Currently, global quantum science is advancing rapidly. On one hand, the development of quantum computing technology is significantly driving the progress of quantum communication. Quantum computing, as a new mode of computation utilizing the principles of quantum mechanics, leverages the superposition properties of quantum states to achieve parallel computing beyond the capabilities of traditional computers. Quantum computing is of practical significance in realizing quantum cryptography, quantum communication, and quantum computers. It has become a focus of research in intelligent information processing, particularly in information security, with broad application prospects. The notion that quantum computers will be the next generation of computers is increasingly accepted in the industry.

Quantum technology has made progress in cognitive science and an attempt to mimic human learning methods in engineering systems, serving to build systems that represent and mimic human intelligence. Photonic quantum chips, characterized by their high processing speed and small size, can be applied in the manufacturing of nanoscale robots, various electronic devices, and embedded technologies.

Moreover, its application scope includes large-scale equipment like satellite vehicles and nuclear energy control, neutrino communication technology, quantum communication technology, virtual space communication technology in information transmission, advanced military high-tech weapons, and new medical technologies in high-end scientific research domains, offering enormous market potential. With breakthroughs in quantum storage capabilities, the development of quantum computing technology, and the application of quantum error correction coding and quantum detection technologies, the efficiency of quantum communication systems will be significantly enhanced.

On the other hand, quantum communication is moving toward large-scale applications, transitioning from private to public networks. Quantum communication technology, a fundamental means to ensure information security, holds significant economic and strategic value. Its long-term goal is to achieve absolute secure long-distance quantum communication, ultimately promoting the industrialization of quantum secure communication. The practical application of quantum communication, from principle to addressing specific problems on a small scale, is a global endeavor.

However, further exploration is needed on integrating quantum communication systems into classical communication networks and balancing cost and benefit to realize true quantum communication networks. According to the roadmap of the quantum communication network system, the practical application of quantum communication technology will proceed in three steps: first, regional quantum communication networks through optical fibers; second, urban quantum communication networks through quantum repeaters; and third, global quantum communication networks covering the entire globe through satellite relay.

Currently, quantum communication research has entered a critical period of engineering realization. With the industrialization of quantum communication technology and the realization of wide-area quantum communication networks, quantum communication, as a key technology to ensure future information society communication security, is expected to move toward large-scale application within the next ten years. It will become a driver for various electronic services such as e-government, e-commerce, e-health, biometric transmission, and intelligent transmission systems, providing fundamental security services and the most reliable security guarantee for today's information society.

Moreover, quantum communication has significant application value and prospects in the military, national defense, finance, and other information security domains. It can be used for national-level confidential communication in military and defense areas, government, telecommunications, securities, insurance, banking, industrial and commercial, local taxation, financial, and other sectors and departments involving secret data and bills. Quantum communication can be used for both civilian and military purposes. If paired with satellite devices, its application fields will be even broader, more numerous, and deeper. Once quantum communication satellites succeed, they will unveil a new chapter in the information technology industry. Not only will it completely transform traditional information industries, but it will also promote emerging information industries, including computing, software, satellite communication, databases, consulting services, audio-visual, information system construction, and more, making them more efficient, faster, and more secure.

In addition, the space race for quantum satellites will also unfold competitively. Although the quantum communication industry is still in its early stages of development, it has already found widespread application in satellite communication and space technology. This provides a new solution for global quantum communication, namely, through the combination of quantum storage technology and quantum entanglement exchange and purification technology to create quantum repeaters, breaking the limitations of short-distance fiber optic and terrestrial free-space communication, extending quantum communication distances, and achieving true global quantum communication.

Countries capable of quantum satellite transmission will gain many new advantages, including encrypting highly sensitive secrets. All concerned countries compete to develop relevant technologies to gain the upper hand in quantum communication. Currently, many research teams worldwide are constructing quantum transmission devices that can be carried by satellites, and the space race for quantum satellites will occur among various nations.

With the development of quantum technology, it is foreseeable that it will give rise to a series of important commercial and defense applications, bringing lucrative market opportunities and disruptive military capabilities.

TOWARD QUANTUM WORLD

8.1 Quantum Revolution beyond Imagination

Since Max Planck introduced the concept of the "quantum" over a century ago, Quantum science has undergone a vast and dramatic evolution. Often divided into two stages, "the first quantum technological revolution" and "the second quantum technological revolution," we are currently in the midst of the second. Looking into the distant future, the breakthroughs achieved in this second revolution may surpass human imagination, leading us toward previously unimagined realms.

8.1.1 The Four Revolutions in Physics

The journey of physics has seen multiple theoretical upheavals and practical innovations. Each revolution in physics has introduced new technologies and reshaped our worldview.

The first revolution was Newton's mechanical revolution. Newton unified two seemingly unrelated natural phenomena: the movement of planets in the night sky and the fall of apples to the ground. He explained these disparate phenomena using the theory of universal gravitation and mechanics. More importantly, Newton proposed a worldview for understanding everything: all matter consists of particles, and the motion of these particles adheres to Newton's laws. This made Newtonian mechanics a universal theory for understanding the natural world, marking the dawn of the era of classical mechanics.

The second revolution was Maxwell's electromagnetic revolution. Maxwell successfully unified electricity, magnetism, and light in this period—three seemingly unrelated physical phenomena. He first formulated Maxwell's equations, perfectly describing the behavior of electric and magnetic fields, thereby unifying electromagnetic phenomena. Further research revealed that the wave speed of electromagnetic waves, as described by Maxwell's equations, was nearly identical to the measured speed of light. Consequently, Maxwell proposed that electromagnetic waves are light, unifying electricity, magnetism, and light. The essence of the second revolution was the discovery of wave-like matter.

The third revolution was Einstein's theory of relativity. Einstein pointed out that gravitational effects stem from the warping of spacetime. On a deeper level, the relativistic revolution discovered a second form of matter—gravitational waves, which are fluctuations in the warping of spacetime.

The fourth revolution is the quantum revolution. The Quantum revolution is deeply profound in the history of physics. However, it was not the work of a single individual; rather, it was a collective achievement of a large group of physicists. In 1927, the fifth Solvay Conference was held in Brussels, where 29 top scientists from around the world, including older generation scientists like Niels Bohr, Arnold Sommerfeld, Wolfgang Pauli, Albert Einstein, and the younger generation represented by Heisenberg, Dirac, and Schrödinger, gathered. The theories they presented at this conference profoundly influenced the evolution and development of quantum mechanics for over half a century. The "wave mechanics" represented by Schrödinger, the "matrix mechanics" and "uncertainty principle" represented by Heisenberg, and Dirac's "Dirac equation" and "quantum radiation theory" provided important theoretical support for the development of quantum mechanics.

The quantum revolution overturned many of humanity's previous understandings. According to the principles of quantum mechanics, the world itself is a game of chance. All matter in the universe consists of atoms and subatomic particles, and probability, not certainty, governs atoms and subatomic particles. Fundamentally, the theory of quantum mechanics posits that nature is built on randomness, which is counterintuitive to human perception. Moreover, quantum mechanics encompasses many counterintuitive concepts, such as Schrödinger's cat being both dead and alive, faster-than-light quantum entanglement, and quantum tunneling akin to walking through walls.

Despite sounding bizarre and absurd, quantum mechanics is a theory solidly grounded in objective phenomena, and both its experimental precision and theoretical accuracy are incredibly high. It may be the most accurate of all scientific theories to date. Richard Feynman once used an example to illustrate this precision. In quantum electrodynamics, the theoretical calculation of the electron's anomalous magnetic moment is so precise that the error compared to the actual experimental measurement is akin to the difference of a hair's breadth between New York and Los Angeles. This speaks volumes about the accuracy of quantum mechanics.

8.1.2 The Second Quantum Revolution Has Arrived

The history of quantum mechanics is tumultuous and grand, often divided into two phases: "the first quantum technological revolution" and "the second quantum technological revolution."

The "first quantum technological revolution" began in the early 20th century when physicists faced phenomena that classical physics could not explain, such as blackbody radiation. Unable to explain blackbody radiation with classical physics, Max Planck innovatively proposed the concept of the "quantum," suggesting that electromagnetic waves radiating from a blackbody are emitted in discrete amounts, each of which he called a "quantum." Planck's idea of quantized energy broke the fundamental classical physics assumption of continuously variable physical quantities, proposing the notion of discrete energy states, and thus opened the door to the quantum world.

Building on Planck's concept that energy is not continuous but quantized and related to frequency, Einstein hypothesized that if energy is discrete, and since light is a form of electromagnetic wave, then perhaps light is also not continuous. This is the "light quantum" hypothesis. Einstein's hypothesis on light quanta solved the photoelectric effect problem and further laid the foundation of quantum theory. Despite Einstein's photoelectric effect being a key step in exploring the quantum world, he appeared later as an opponent in developing quantum mechanics.

The first quantum technological revolution ended in the late 20th century. During this period, physicists completed the framework of quantum mechanics, describing its basic features. This era brought numerous technological innovations related to quantum theory, such as nuclear energy, semiconductors, lasers, NMR, high-temperature superconductors, and giant magnetoresistance. Quantum mechanics became the hardware foundation of modern information technology, with mathematics as its software foundation laying the groundwork for all modern information technology.

In fact, many results of basic research related to quantum mechanics can be seen in everyday items, like semiconductors and integrated circuits in smartphones.

The development of semiconductors led to modern computers; then, with massive data transmission worldwide, the Internet was born. Atomic clocks, precision instruments of quantum mechanics, were invented to verify relativity, aiding global satellite navigation. It can be said that the first quantum revolution directly spurred modern information technology.

However, the first quantum technological revolution needed to be more thorough. This is because, fundamentally, it was just a quantum material revolution involving only operational applications of atoms, electrons, and photons without fully utilizing quantum theory's laws, such as quantum superposition, entanglement, etc. Additionally, the first revolution left many fundamental issues unresolved, including measurement problems, the divide between micro and macro (classical and quantum boundaries), and understanding the essence of quantum entanglement. These foundational issues left many puzzles in quantum theory.

On this basis, human society welcomed the second quantum technological revolution. If the first revolution represented humanity's passive observation and application of quantum rules, then the second is about active control and manipulation of quantum states. Currently, the main development area in this second revolution is quantum information technology, with the three main fields being quantum computing, quantum communication, and quantum precision measurement. Quantum information technology has significantly advanced in principles, content, and value compared to traditional information technology.

Specifically, the second quantum revolution has achieved direct manipulation of quantum objects and fully utilizes the fundamental laws of quantum mechanics. Technologies such as lasers and semiconductors from the first revolution still adhered to classical physics, only involving quantum mechanical laws under certain conditions. These devices couldn't directly control individual particles or involve quantum basics like entanglement and non-locality. The second revolution, with technologies like quantum computers, is entirely based on quantum principles.

Moreover, humanity is no longer a passive observer of the quantum world but actively uses quantum mechanics to change life. Previously, humans could understand and explain the microscopic world with quantum mechanics, like explaining the periodic table, but couldn't actively design artificial atoms or manipulate their behavior. Now, with the second quantum revolution, humans actively use quantum mechanics to alter the quantum face of the physical world. We can now design and create new artificial atoms with preselected electronic and optical properties and fabricate new artificial quantum states with coherence or entanglement, which have wide applications in computers, communication systems, sensors, and compact metrology devices.

The quantum revolution has undergone a long period of theoretical preparation and holds vast technological potential. While we can't predict all applications the second quantum revolution will bring, early-stage quantum communication and computing breakthroughs have already shown quantum information technology's significant value and broad prospects.

As the second quantum revolution progresses, quantum technology will burst forth, changing existing ways of life and even affecting global dynamics. Imagine the accelerated development of AI and the advancement of deep learning and neural networks when quantum computing merges with blockchain, big data, cloud computing, AI, cryptocurrencies, smart manufacturing, and the IoT. The complex molecular simulations made possible by quantum technology could change the course of human destiny.

Humanity has entered an era where quantum mechanics and quantum technology are intimately linked to everyone. In the future, the digital transformation of global traditional industries will incorporate quantum factors. A quantum industrial system and ecosystem are quietly forming around quantum computing, quantum communication, and quantum networks.

8.2   Reshaping Worldviews

The quantum revolution is as much a profound intellectual transformation as it is a disruptive technological upheaval.

From the onset of quantum mechanics, doubts and debates about its theories have been relentless. Nonetheless, quantum mechanics continues to flourish, with new laws being discovered and validated and our understanding of its principles ever-expanding. The deepening exploration into quantum mechanics has led to a broader familiarity with its scientific content and sparked intense interest. More than just delving into physics, quantum science is reshaping our worldview.

8.2.1 The Disappearance of Causality

The philosophical reflections stirred by quantum science are manifold, rooted fundamentally in the stark differences between the quantum world and the macroscopic world.

Before quantum science, our view of causality was straightforward: a cause leads to an effect, and a specific cause corresponds to a specific effect. For instance, it's like having only one road from the office to home. If I wait patiently on this road, I'm certain to meet you. This unyielding causal relationship offered great convenience: we could deduce causes from known effects to solve problems, and if we desired a particular outcome, we simply had to follow the required causes. For example, gaining weight due to overeating implies that eating less will lead to weight loss. However, quantum science sees things differently. In the quantum world, nothing is certain; only probabilities describe things.

In the macroscopic world, there's only one path from home to school; waiting on this path ensures our meeting. In the quantum world, there are many paths from home to school; waiting somewhere only gives a probability of meeting. Before quantum science, our judgments about causality were definite. But with the advent of quantum science, the world became indeterminate.

Quantum science doesn't only unsettle our notions of causality; it also provides a basis for phenomena considered mystical, like telepathy. Under quantum entanglement theory, if two particles are entangled, regardless of distance, a change in one particle results in a corresponding change in the other. Thus, manipulating one particle's state could control the others. This implies that despite vast distances, two particles can maintain a certain relationship.

The principle of quantum entanglement suggests the existence of a force causing distant objects to react in unison, influencing a person's actions due to another person's behavior, akin to telepathy. Although telepathy has been a topic of interest despite its stretched interpretations, quantum entanglement theory offers a plausible explanation, provoking philosophical contemplation.

Moreover, classical and quantum worldviews clash in their conceptions of space and time. In classical views, every event occupies a definite position in space and occurs at a specific moment. Ludwig Boltzmann first defined time by using entropy to explain the second law of thermodynamics. He described entropy as a measure of system disorder, stating that entropy can only increase, not decrease, with the minimum entropy being zero. According to thermodynamics, the entropy of all isolated systems spontaneously increases, giving time a "directional arrow." Simply put, time is linear.

However, quantum theory posits that time, as we define it, may not truly exist. Using time to explain everything is bound to encounter inexplicable situations. Quantum entanglement, for example, defies temporal and spatial explanations. When two entangled particles are separated across vast distances, changes in one particle instantaneously reflect in the other, defying the physical constraints of time and space.

Supposing time and space don't exist, the entire universe is an integrated whole. The distance between two particles is merely a human perception; in reality, they remain entangled within a unified system. Thus, their information transfer or synchronicity can occur instantaneously. This resembles looking in a mirror: the "reflection" is entangled with the "physical self," moving synchronously and oppositely without needing information transfer, as they are just two aspects of the same entity. Ideal mirror reflections create an infinitely large space, even larger than the universe.

If our universe is the mirror image of an actual universe, then time and distance lose their meaning. The movements of two entangled objects (mirrors) are synchronous and opposite, without requiring information communication. They are merely two images of the same entity. Quantum theory introduces a new concept of space-time, challenging our understanding as our measurements of space and time are based on human perspectives. Our reference to macroscopic and microscopic worlds also relies on a human scale. But the world is not made of humans; it comprises "microscopic" particles. We can fundamentally understand the universe's logic only by perfectly explaining the physical laws of the microscopic world. This is the value of researching quantum laws.

The quantum world provokes diverse and varying thoughts across disciplines. Through these discussions and considerations, we gradually clear the fog and glimpse a more exciting and clear world.

8.2.2 Developing Quantum Thinking

The evolution of quantum theory has unveiled a new facet of our world, leading to the emergence of a novel scientific worldview and approach: quantum thinking.

Distinct from traditional classical physics, quantum thinking embraces a holistic perspective. Classical physics, one of humanity's most significant intellectual contributions, taught us to decompose complex phenomena into modular components, viewing the whole as the sum of its parts and the world as a composition of independent entities. This approach, when applied industrially, led to breaking down complex manufacturing processes into simple tasks that were executed mechanically, boosting production efficiency and resulting in unprecedented wealth creation during the post-Industrial Revolution era. We dissected plant growth elements in agriculture, enhancing them with chemical compounds for targeted pest control and weed elimination. Our growing expertise in disassembling has even extended to deconstructing seeds into numerous genes, producing pest-resistant cotton and protein-rich, high-yield soybeans.

In the classical mechanical world, everything is divisible and measurable. However, the quantum world defies this notion. Quantum theory posits that the universe contains no independent, fixed entities; it comprises dynamic energy patterns that interact and superimpose within a "continuous holistic pattern." The world is intricately interconnected, requiring a holistic view where the whole generates and determines the parts, and the parts also contain information about the whole.

Viewing agriculture through quantum theory, the ecosystem of crops forms a circular whole, interdependent and mutually nurturing. Simplistically seen through Newtonian thinking, insects harm crops; thus, exterminating insects seems a direct solution. However, this contradicts the philosophical concept of mutual generation and restraint, akin to the Five Elements theory, where the absence of one element disrupts the entire cycle.

Similar holistic concepts exist in Confucianism, Taoism, and Buddhism. Confucius's idea of "penetrating unity," Wang Yangming's lifelong advocacy of "all things as one," and his teachings like "the mind is the principle," "unity of knowledge and action," and "attaining good conscience" reflect this. The "all things as one" theme was central in Wang Yangming's later teachings, repeatedly elucidated in writings like "Response to Gu Dongqiao."

Laozi's *Tao Te Ching* speaks of unity in phrases like "The sages who grasped the One became models for the world" and "The *Tao* gives birth to One, One to Two, Two to Three, Three to all things. All things carry *Yin* and embrace *Yang*, achieving harmony through these energies." These are expressions of universal unity.

Buddha's *Diamond Sutra* states, "If the world exists, then this is a unified whole. The Tathagata speaks of a unified whole, which is not a unified whole, and this is called a unified whole." The *Shurangama Sutra* explains the illusory nature of our perceptions and the unity of all phenomena.

The *Heart Sutra*'s phrase "Form is emptiness, emptiness is form" might be the most fitting interpretation of quantum mechanics, transcending traditional classical physics. Quantum thinking redefines our understanding of causality, space-time, and the universe's interconnectedness, reshaping our worldview profoundly.

In discussing postmodern science and the world, British physicist David Bohm noted that "although there are many differences between relativity and quantum physics, they are united in the aspect of a complete whole."

Moreover, quantum thinking is characterized by its diversity. Quantum theory proposes that the world is "plural," filled with diversity and multiple choices, urging us to observe and interpret the world and its phenomena not in a binary "either-or" manner but in a more inclusive, "both-and" approach. Diversity implies that before making any decision, the possibilities are infinite and variable, only collapsing into a single outcome once a choice is made. This reflects the non-linear nature of quantum systems, often in states of chaos, evolving through quantum leaps. Small inputs can significantly disrupt these chaotic states, exemplified by the "butterfly effect."

Finally, quantum thinking involves embracing uncertainty. Classical physics views biological evolution as following a specific law, suggesting a predictable development of all things. Quantum physics, however, suggests the opposite: both the environment and the internal dynamics of quantum systems embody "uncertainty." Heisenberg's Uncertainty Principle states, "We cannot simultaneously study a particle's position and momentum; we can only measure one at a time." This encompasses two aspects: first, focusing on the part of a whole inherently isolates it, selectively discarding other possibilities. Our inquiries and measurements choose only one aspect of a quantum system, ignoring other factors and possibilities. Second, every interaction with a quantum system alters it. Under this principle, biological evolution can be understood as the outcome of numerous random coincidences, turning inorganic matter into cells, organic matter, and eventually humans, implying that the development of all things is random and unpredictable.

This means we need both traditional and quantum thinking to understand the world. Quantum thinking differs fundamentally from classical physics, offering a more comprehensive and flexible way of thinking.

Once remote, quantum mechanics is now intimately linked with our understanding of the physical world. A century ago, our grasp of physics was empirical; in the 20th century, quantum mechanics provided a theory of matter and fields, altering our world. In the 21st century, quantum mechanics will continue to furnish fundamental concepts and essential tools for all sciences.

We stand at the threshold of the quantum era. As the world surfs waves of rapid change, the swift growth of quantum technology continuously transforms everyday life. The quest for perfection in technology and science becomes a trend, and quantum technology, no longer a niche term, emerges as a dynamic and evolving ideology. Whatever the outcome, the dream of an ultimate understanding of nature, born at the dawn of science, will persist as a driving force for new knowledge. In the future, quantum technology will lead us beyond limitations toward a broader horizon.

As we witness the dawn of quantum technology, scientists strive to empirically define its portrait, attempting to solidify it or make it replicable and controllable industrially. The quantum technology we harness today may not fully represent true quantum mechanics; it might be a form closer to quantum technology, transcending classical physics. Regardless, this advanced form of quantum technology already reveals a magical power—a technology of immense potential.

REFERENCES

Bohm, D. *Quantum Theory*. Translated by Hou Depeng.

Cheng, Sumei. *Dialogue between Science and Philosophy*.

China Academy of Information and Communications Technology. *Quantum Information Technology Development and Application Research Report*. 2020.

China Communications Society. *Frontier Report on Quantum Confidential Communication Technology Development and Application*. 2020.

Ding, Ling. "A Survey of Quantum Machine Learning Algorithms." *Electronics World*, no. 12 (Dec. 2019): 24–26. doi:10.19353/j.cnki.dzsj.

Dongwu Securities. *In-Depth Study of Quantum Communication and Quantum Computing Industry*.

Gao, Peng, Zhou Huaxu, Yu Guoji, et al. "Quantum Communication Technology and Current Application Analysis." *Electronic Design Engineering* 28, no. 16 (Jun. 2020): 115–118, 123. doi:10.14022/j.issn1674-6236.

Guo, Yiling, and Shen Huijun. *History of Physics*.

Hao, Qiaoli, Zhao Yanqiang, Li Yinjie. "Analysis of the Global Development Trend of Quantum Sensing." *World Science and Technology Research and Development* 44, no. 01 (Oct. 2022): 59–68. doi:10.16507/j.issn.1006-6055.

Huaan Securities. *In-Depth Report on Quantum Technology: Breaking the Spear of Moore's Law, Guarding the Shield of Information Security*. 2022.

Huang, HsinYuan, Broughton Michael, Cotler Jordan, et al. "Quantum Advantage in Learning from Experiments." *Science (New York, N.Y.)* (2022).

Huang, Yiming, Lei Hang, Li Xiaoyu. "A Survey of Quantum Machine Learning Algorithms." *Chinese Journal of Computers* 41, no. 01 (2018): 145–163.

Guangda Securities. *Prospect and Market Analysis of Quantum Computing and Quantum Communication Technologies*.

Li, Xiaowei, Fu Xiang, Yan Fei, et al. "Current Status and Future Development of Quantum Computing Research." *Engineering Sciences* 24, no. 04 (2022): 133–144.

Lin, Youbin. "Application and Prospects of Quantum Communication Technology." *Electronics Technology* 51, no. 02 (2022): 18–19.

Long, Guiru. "Research and Future Prospects of Quantum Computers." *People's Forum—Academic Frontiers*, no. 07 (July 2021): 44–56. doi:10.16619/j.cnki. rmltxsqy.

Morishita, H., Tashima T., Mima D., Kato H., Makino T., Yamasaki S., Fujiwara M., et al. "Extension of the Coherence Time by Generating MW Dressed States in a Single NV Centre in Diamond." *Scientific Reports* (2019).

Photon Box. *Global Quantum Communications Industry Development Report.* 2022.

Photon Box. *Global Quantum Precision Measurement Industry Development Report.* 2022.

Photon Box. *Quantum Technology Panorama Outlook.* 2021.

Photon Box. *Quantum Technology Panorama Outlook: Quantum Hardware, Algorithms, Software, Internet.* 2022.

Qiao, Lingai, and Wei Quanxiang. "Einstein's Significant Impact on the Development of Quantum Theory." *University Physics*, no. 05 (May 2006): 48–52. doi:10.16854/j.cnki.1000-0712.

Román, Orús, Samuel Mugel, and Enrique Lizaso. "Quantum Computing for Finance: Overview and Prospects." *Reviews in Physics* (2019).

"The Emergence of 'Jiuzhang,' Achieving a Milestone of 'Quantum Computing Supremacy.'" *International Talent Exchange*, no. 01 (2021): 58–59.

Wang, Xiangbin, and Pan Jianwei. "The 2022 Nobel Prize in Physics: Quantum Entanglement." *China Science Foundation* 36, no. 06 (Jun. 2022): 928–930. doi:10.16262/j.cnki.1000-8217.

Wang, Yongli, and Xu Qiuliang. "Overview of the Principles and Research Progress of Quantum Computing and Quantum Cryptography." *Journal of Computer Research and Development* 57, no. 10 (2020): 2015–2026.

Yang, Shuwei, and Liu Guoyu. "The Birth and Development of Quantum Theory—From Quantum Theory to Quantum Mechanics." *Radio and TV University of Science and Technology*, no. 01 (2015): 30–31.

Yuan, Aifang, and Liu Didi. "Analysis of the Uncertainty Principle in Quantum Mechanics." *University Physics* 30, no. 11 (Nov. 2011): 44–49. doi:10.16854/j. cnki.1000-0712.

Zhang, Wei. "Embracing the Era of Quantum Technology: The Status Quo and Prospects of Quantum Computing." *People's Forum—Academic Frontiers*, no. 07 (July 2021): 64–75. doi:10.16619/j.cnki.rmltxsqy.

Zhong, Hansen, Wang Hui, Deng Yuhao, Chen Mingcheng, Peng Lichao, Luo Yihan, Qin Jian, et al. "Quantum Computational Advantage Using Photons." *Science (New York, N.Y.)* (2020).

Zhongyuan Securities. *Special Report on Quantum Information Industry: Layout of Quantum Information, Starting the Future of Information Technology.*

INDEX

Y

Young, Thomas, 30–31

Young's double-slit experiment, 30–31

Z

Zeilinger, Anton, 108

Zeilinger group, 120

Zoller, Peter, 81

ZTE, 130

ABOUT THE AUTHOR

Kevin Chen is a renowned science and technology writer and scholar. He was a visiting scholar at Columbia University, a postdoctoral scholar at the University of Cambridge, and an invited course professor at Peking University. He has served as a special commentator and columnist for the *People's Daily*, CCTV, China Business Network, SINA, NetEase, and many other media outlets. He has published monographs in numerous domains, including finance, science and technology, real estate, medical treatments, and industrial design. He currently lives in Hong Kong.